An OPUS book

THE STATE AND THE ECONOMIC SYSTEM

OPUS General Editors

Keith Thomas
Alan Ryan
Walter Bodmer

OPUS books provide concise, original, and authoritative introductions to a wide range of subjects in the humanities and sciences. They are written by experts for the general reader as well as for students.

The State and the Economic System

An Introduction to the History of Political Economy

PHYLLIS DEANE

Oxford   New York

OXFORD UNIVERSITY PRESS

1989

Oxford University Press, Walton Street, Oxford OX2 6DP

Oxford New York Toronto
Delhi Bombay Calcutta Madras Karachi
Petaling Jaya Singapore Hong Kong Tokyo
Nairobi Dar es Salaam Cape Town
Melbourne Auckland

and associated companies in
Berlin Ibadan

Oxford is a trade mark of Oxford University Press

British Library Cataloguing in Publication Data
Deane, Phyllis
The state and the economic system: an introduction to the history
of political economy. —(OPUS).
1. Economics, to 1986
I. Title   II. Series
330'.09
ISBN 0-19-219187-X
ISBN 0-19-289169-3   Pbk

Library of Congress Cataloging in Publication Data
Deane, Phyllis.
The state and the economic system: an introduction to the history
of political economy/Phyllis Deane.
p.   cm. — (OPUS)
Bibliography: p.   Includes index.
1. Economics.   2. Economic policy.   I. Title.   II. Series.
HB171.D34 1989 338.9—dc19 88-4217
ISBN 0-19-219187-X
ISBN 0-19-289169-3 (pbk.)

Set by Colset Private Ltd.

Printed in Great Britain by
The Guernsey Press Co. Ltd.
Guernsey, Channel Islands

Preface

The search for systematic regularities in economic behaviour that motivates the scientific activity called political economy—now commonly referred to as economics—originated in response to the information needs of central government policy-makers. Today, in spite of the sophisticated analytical techniques, and often highly esoteric specialisms characterizing late twentieth-century economic science, the primary object of the exercise remains the same as it was in the seventeenth century: to provide national administrators and their responsible agents with the objective knowledge needed to design and implement efficient economic policies. I have retained the old-fashioned title for the discipline in order to emphasize its perennial political dimension rather than to conjure up any of the ideological overtones that some modern users of the term have attached to it. In this book, that is to say, political economy is synonymous with economics and my focus is on the interface between what seventeenth-century writers on economic affairs would have called the polity (the civil order of society) and the economy.

The body of knowledge covered by this subject is wide, and those who are in some sense qualified to advance, teach, or apply its principles also range over an exceedingly broad spectrum of professional analysts. Partly because of its breadth and the variety of its practitioners and partly, because its problems and its findings are usually highly specific in time and place, the precepts and prescriptions offered by orthodox economic doctrine lack the certainty or authority expected of most sciences of equivalent maturity. One result is that politicians, or voters, who need to assess the probable efficiency of alternative economic policies rarely find a consensus among experts, even on quite narrow economic issues, still less on problems that raise significant social or ideological considerations. The apparent lack of absolute conviction with which economic advice is usually offered may be compounded by the fact that the leading professionals who are seen by their peers as actively pushing back the frontiers of objective economic knowledge in their specialisms tend to be more pragmatic than dogmatic in their approach to their researches or analyses. In so far as they have a concern with practical economic policy problems—as even the purest of pure theorists generally do—they are moreover at least as strongly influenced by the contemporary background of general ideas and attitudes that constitute the spirit of the age in which they operate as they are by the accumulated wisdom of economic science.

My purpose in writing this deliberately slim volume is not to provide a formal history of economic theory or analysis from a twentieth-century perspective. Instead I have set out to sketch the development of economic knowledge over the past three hundred years with particular reference to the ways in which the broader context of moral, scientific, and political ideas or events have influenced successive economists' vision of the operations of the changing economic system and their views of the scope for purposive State action to shape the process of change. It is rather heavily documented by quotations from primary sources and highly selective in its choice of topics and individuals for discussion. Considerations of space have encouraged me to focus on a limited number of well-known (largely but not exclusively) British individuals and policy problems, although many of the points I wanted to make might have been as well illustrated by reference to other thinkers or political contexts. In short, this book is offered as a starting-point for further thought and discussion rather than as a set of final conclusions. As such I hope it will prove of interest not only to students of economics and of ideas generally, but also to that wider educated public which needs to evaluate the nature and usefulness of the science of political economy.

I am grateful to innumerable scholars on whose published researches I have drawn without acknowledgement in writing this book; to Dr G. C. Harcourt, my friend and colleague, who found time to read the typescript and rescue me from certain errors of fact and judgement; to Jenny Woodhouse and her team at the University of Cambridge Faculty of Economics for getting the last of the typescripts into press-worthy form; and to the editors of Oxford University Press for their remedial work on my literary style.

PHYLLIS DEANE
January 1988

Contents

1

Prelude to the origins of political economy

The origins of modern political economy as a distinct system of objective knowledge, a branch of moral or political science, can be traced back to the seventeenth century. Long before that the educated élite of Europe had been concerned with ethical and practical issues of economic policy, and there already existed a substantial analytical or empirical literature focused on economic questions of a kind that still face modern economists. Aristotle, for example, had been motivated by a concern with the ethics of pricing to analyse the practice of market exchange and to develop a rudimentary theory of money. St Thomas Aquinas, writing in the thirteenth century, at a later stage in the development of the exchange economy, was also concerned with problems of formulating ethical criteria for the market-place when he discussed the concept of the just price and condemned usury. Later still, in the sixteenth century, the expansion of international commerce, the growth in the authority of centralized nation-states, the social and cultural dislocation resulting from the Reformation, and the development of capitalistic techniques of economic organization combined to demonstrate to both rulers and ruled the urgent need for, and the opportunities inherent in, well-informed *national* economic policies.

Accordingly, there emerged from the new printing presses a swelling stream of tracts and pamphlets designed to offer advice to administrators on questions of public finance and on agricultural, or commercial, or industrial development, as well as on the perennial problems of price inflation, economic recession and poverty, and these owed little to the traditional theological doctrine or canon law on which the medieval schoolmen had sought to base their criteria. It was under the influence of the new view of the universe and of men's position in it—a new view associated with the scientific revolution of the seventeenth century—that the study of political economy began to acquire some of the characteristics of a scientific discipline.

The need to articulate systematic explanations for the behaviour patterns of individuals operating in the market-place became progressively more urgent as trade and industry developed, and as national governments extended the range of their responsibilities in European economies. As long as the typical unit of production was primarily occupied in meeting family subsistence needs, and was operating with traditional techniques within a custom-dominated framework of personal rights and obligations, the scope for individual decision-making in relation to either prices or production was severely limited. In these circumstances, writers on economic questions were primarily concerned to prescribe ethical and political rules designed to ensure a just system of interpersonal relations. There was little scope for more than rudimentary exercises in economic analysis. Scholastic theologians and jurists, for example, favoured competition and opposed monopolistic or discriminatory trading practices, on the grounds that a free market (modified where justice demanded by public regulation of prices or wages) was most likely to lead to a socially acceptable structure of prices and incomes. In a world where sustained improvements in output or productivity or standards of living were at best barely perceptible, and where one individual's or nation's gain from trade seemed to mark another's loss, the ruthless pursuit of individual advantage in the market-place was hard to justify.

Thus Martin Luther was expressing the social consensus of an economically static pre-capitalist era when he condemned usury as a mortal sin, and advocated that traders should always charge a just price for their wares. To those who sought guidance on how to calculate a just price he advised, first and foremost, respect for the regulations laid down by governmental authorities: '. . . the best and safest way would be for the temporal authorities to appoint over this matter wise and honest men who would appraise the cost of all sorts of wares and fix accordingly the outside price at which the merchant would get his due and have an honest living.' But since such price regulation was not always practicable, 'the next best thing is to hold our wares at the price which they bring in the common market or which is customary in the neighbourhood. In this matter we can accept the proverb "Do like others and you are no fool".' Finally, in cases where neither law nor custom have set a clear price, his advice was: '. . . you must make up your minds to seek in your trading only your honest living, count your costs, trouble, labour and risk on that basis, and then fix, raise or lower the price of your goods so that you are paid for your trouble and labour.'

In the century after Luther's death, however, the context of economic ideas was transformed by the cumulative consequences of three revolutionary developments. The first was the Reformation, in which he was himself one of the prime movers. The second was a revolution in the scientific world view which Luther had reacted against by dismissing Copernicus as the fool who wanted to reverse the whole science of astronomy. The third was the opening up of the New World, which was to shift the centre of gravity of the European economy towards its north-western regions and to set off a vigorous and cumulative expansion of international trade. These three developments had radical implications for the ethical, political, and epistemological attitudes of those who wrote authoritatively on economic questions.

The last of these developments had the most direct economic consequences, for by enlarging the resource horizons of European countries bordering the Atlantic Ocean it opened up unprecedented opportunities for their merchants to make gains from trade and brought a sharp increase in their supply of monetary metals. There were also political implications. The increasing power and wealth of the merchant classes assured them a privileged position in national economies where they became the natural allies of ambitious sixteenth-century monarchs intent on establishing their supremacy over temporal and spiritual lords on the one hand and foreign powers on the other.

The politico-economic repercussions of the Reformation were various. They played a particularly significant role in shaping capitalist national economies. Victory in the long struggle for dominance between the Roman Church and rulers of individual nation states increased both the political authority and the economic responsibilities of central government and altered the distribution of national wealth. In England, for example, the state hastily sold off the confiscated church estates, spending the proceeds as if they represented additions to its income rather than capital resources, with the result that after a decade or so of sharp speculation on the land market the church properties were largely acquired by a new class of landowners, who set out to manage them according to capitalist rather than feudal rules of the game. Thus it turned out that the dissolution of monasteries added more to the national stock of negotiable wealth than the treasure brought back by English privateers who harried Spanish ships, for it moved a substantial slab of national wealth away from the religious institutions whose objectives were essentially concerned with consumption rather than production and into the hands of owners eager to maximize their money incomes by using their capital assests as productively as possible. Equally as important, however, if less easily located in time and space, was the change in ethical attitudes that stemmed from the Reformation.

After Luther (a peasant mystic imbued with the traditional economic ethic of an agrarian community) Protestant doctrine became steadily more worldly and rationalistic and correspondingly more sympathetic to the selfish values of an acquisitive individualistic society. The Genevan Calvin, for example, lived in a city which had already reached an advanced level of commercial organization and he viewed the profits earned in trade and industry as a just reward for entrepreneurial diligence and care in pursuit of God-given callings. Puritanism was less urban in its orientation, but the Puritan divines followed the Calvinists in stressing the virtues of frugality and of unflagging commitment to a vocation and they approved money-making activities generally—provided that the fruits were applied to the glory of God rather than dissipated in personal consumption; and this, in a world where the beggar tended increasingly to be condemned for idleness, was generally interpreted as an argument for ploughing profits back into the business. In Max Weber's picturesque phrase, the Puritan 'stood at the cradle of the economic man'.

The other revolutionary development, which had appeared in educated discourse before the end of the sixteenth century and had a pervasive impact on politico-economic attitudes in the course of the seventeenth century, was a fundamental change in people's perception of their physical environment. It had links with the Reformation as well as with the Renaissance. The Protestant reaction against the ritualism of the Catholic Church merged with a rationalist tradition borrowed from the ancients to stimulate new perspectives on the nature of the universe. The medieval view started from the presumption that the natural world existed only to further man's knowledge, purpose, and destiny and that the earth was the centre of the universe. It was Copernicus' discovery that the Ptolemaic, geocentric theory of the universe had not been accepted uncritically by the ancients that encouraged him to develop his theory of a heliocentric universe. However, it was three decades before he actually published *De revolutionibus orbium coelestium* (1543) and it was not until after Galileo, Kepler, and finally Newton produced the decisive empirical justification for the Copernican theory that it became established as orthodox scientific doctrine. Meanwhile, it was significant that in 1616 the Vatican put *De revolutionibus* on its list of prohibited books and that in 1633 Galileo was brought to trial by the Inquisition and coerced into denying the Copernican system he had helped to justify. By then, however, he had laid the foundations of the new scientific methodology: (1) by clearly distinguishing between the real, objective, mathematically observable world and the subjective, relative world of opinion and illusion, and (2) by focusing on explaining *how* the universe operated, rather than *why*.

It was within this changing blend of ethical, political, and scientific attitudes that writers who were interested in the causes and consequences of economic events and trends were formulating their explanations and policy prescriptions. From the beginning, monetary problems assumed major importance because it was in this sphere that government currency manipulations could have such unpleasantly disturbing effects for all classes of society, and because a strong groundswell of imperfectly understood economic forces was injecting sustained inflationary pressures into agrarian economies already highly vulnerable to price fluctuations induced by harvest failures and wars. The effects of changes in the value of money on domestic prices and foreign exchanges dislocated the customary patterns of commodity value in ways that were both confusing and distressing. In England there were currency debasements in 1526 and successively in the 1540s and early 1550s, followed by a revaluation in 1566. Meanwhile throughout western Europe an upswing in population combined with the influx of Spanish treasure to fuel the rise in prices and mercantile profits that characterized the sixteenth and early seventeenth centuries. There was a doubling of the price of the English consumer's typical basket of foodstuffs between the 1520s and 1550s and it had doubled again by the 1630s.

By mid-twentieth-century standards the long-term rate of inflation was modest enough, but in the imperfectly integrated national markets of sixteenth-century Europe it exerted a persistent downward pressure on labourers' real wages and inflated the profits of those capitalists (agrarian, mercantile, or industrial) who were able to take advantage of the changing price patterns. In England in 1563 the Elizabethan state was sufficiently worried by the deteriorating conditions of the wage-earning classes to enact a Statute of Artificers giving local Justices of the Peace extensive responsibilities for regulating wage rates and conditions of work or apprenticeship. Meanwhile the increasing number of landless labourers on the one hand and the mounting profits of the entrepreneurial and landowning classes on the other was altering not only the distribution of incomes between rich and poor but also the acceptable rules of the game for the nation's producers.

For the monarchs who now held the reins of temporal and spiritual power in the warring nation states of Europe the overriding political objectives of maintaining law and order at home and national strength abroad involved clear economic objectives. They implied the need to maximize government revenues, to increase national wealth, and to minimize the social discontent that stemmed from associated changes in the distribution of income and wealth. The attempts of Tudor and Stuart governments, for example, to take command of changing economic conditions—whether in the interests of labourers (by wage regulation), of consumers (by quality and food supply controls), of small peasants (by checking forced enclosures), or with a view to diverting some of the gains of an inflationary boom to the national exchequer (by grants of monopolies, taxation, or interventions in the money markets)—ran into increasing resistance from those whose profit-maximizing objectives required freedom from state control. In the event, successful English commercial and industrial entrepreneurs became increasingly identified with the Puritan movement; thus fortified by a heady mix of religious fervour and mounting economic power, they took the battle for economic freedom to civil war, regicide, and a republican commonwealth.

By the late sixteenth and seventeenth centuries, then, the national governments of Europe were grappling with economic and social problems created by an expanding mercantile economy, problems on which jurists and mercantilists were generally better equipped, as well as more interested, to offer advice and opinions than were theologians. Policy-makers needed guidance more on how the contemporary market economy actually operated than on how it *ought* to operate in obedience to the absolute moral principles on which individual Christians might base their criteria for social action. What was urgently required was a system of explanation from a macro-economic perspective and a doctrine of the way the public interest might best be served by economic policies. It was in relation to this need that the mercantilist writers on questions of political economy published their polemical literature. Much of it was ephemeral stuff, designed to analyse a contemporary economic problem and to justify a specific solution. Its common starting point was that the primary objective of national economic policy was to increase the earning power of the nation as a whole; and since most of those who were both strongly motivated to write on these questions and well informed on the way the seventeenth-century market economy worked were actively involved in some aspect of trade or finance, it was not surprising that they tended to the view that the best way to promote national strength was to increase the national share of world trade and monetary resources. To the extent that the mercantilists developed a distinctive common doctrine it was the doctrine that the prime movers in national economic development were the industrial, commercial, and maritime branches of the economy whose advantage lay in their ability to increase the national share of international trade.

In its origins, then, political economy was, as the name suggests, an area of political debate. The leading sixteenth- and seventeenth-century writers on economic matters were political activists or public officials whose objective was to inform, or criticize, or justify specific government economic policies. Late seventeenth-century writers (such as Sir William Petty) who set out to introduce quantitative techniques into economic analysis saw themselves as engaged in the study of 'political arithmetic'. A century later, Adam Smith designated political economy as 'a branch of the science of the statesman or legislature' and his lectures on political economy to Glasgow students fell properly within the scope of a formal course on jurisprudence. Later generations of economists have done their best to detach the science of economics from its political associations, but for the historian of economic thought the political context within which economic ideas have developed has always been crucial in determining their form and direction. It is important, that is to say, to identify not only the analytical arguments with which influential past writers have sought to establish what the economic world is like or ought to be like, but also the political objectives of the authors considered—who, for example, were they trying to convince with their essays in persuasion, and to what end?

In sixteenth-century Europe confidence in the stable, traditional view of the universe and of man's place in it had been profoundly shaken by the combined effects of the Renaissance, the Reformation, the opening up of the New World, the new astronomy of Copernicus, and the invention of printing. A worldview which had seemed beyond dispute had become increasingly questionable. New systems of religious, scientific, and political thought challenged ancient assumptions and prejudices without providing solid foundations for a new consensus. The perception of knowledge itself was changing. Instead of truth being ultimately accessible to scholars who could deduce it from the western textual heritage (the Bible or the texts of classical antiquity), knowledge of what the world is like, or ought to be like, became the subject of an endless quest, a cumulative growth in human understanding to which the scientific observer of physical things and events had at least as much to contribute as the priest or the philosopher.

In the sphere of political thought—especially in its economic aspects—the search for reliable knowledge was further complicated by the realization that the underlying structure of social and economic relationships and attitudes was also in process of change. The development of unified nation states, buttressed by expensive bureaucracies and large, well-armed naval or military forces, was shifting the location of political and economic power within and between European societies. The expansion of the world economy and the growth of population was encouraging the evolution of new forms of business and financial organization associated with the spread of a capitalist spirit of enterprise and causing shifts in the international pattern of economic advantage and opportunity. On the continent of Europe the Reformation unleashed civil and religious wars of a socially disruptive and economically damaging kind. In England the alienation of Church lands by the State set off a mania of land speculation and transformed the psychology of landholding. Everywhere the traditional social and economic mould was cracking and new forms of order were seeking legitimation.

Against this background of social dislocation and economic change, two opposing streams of political theory developed in early modern Europe. On the one hand an absolutist ideology, consistent with the Lutheran perspective on temporal authority, eventually took shape in the doctrine of the 'divine right' of kings. On the other there was the natural-law doctrine emerging from St Thomas Aquinas' vision of a natural law of mankind, ideally enacted by natural communities (that is, commonwealths of basically free and equal individuals) who respected both the divine will and the impersonal forces of nature. This became associated with an ideology of popular sovereignty—the idea that ultimate political authority resides in the body of the people. By the beginning of the seventeenth century these competing ideologies dominated debate on what was becoming the central issue in European political thought: the nature, powers, and rights of the modern State, a State whose legislative authority, claims to allegiance, and social responsibility took precedence over any other rule-making body in society.

In England, a special concatenation of circumstances combined to make the century 1540–1640 one of unprecedented commercial and industrial expansion. They included the long domestic peace of the Tudor era (when the major European powers were torn by religious and dynastic conflicts), the liberation of the Atlantic economy following the defeat of the Spanish Armada, and the locational advantages of an independent seafaring nation lying astride the intercontinental sea routes of what was then the most dynamic region of the world economy—north-western Europe. A century of exposure to this environment of economic change and challenge stimulated the rise of a capitalist class imbued with the intensely individualistic ideology of the successful entrepreneur and enjoying the exercise of the socio-economic power that was associated with a cumulative growth in its share of the nation's material wealth.

As market horizons broadened at national and international levels, the class of capitalist entrepreneurs found its fortunes increasingly vulnerable to the impact of central government economic policy. Well before the end of the sixteenth century the English State (Crown plus Parliament) had established itself as the prime legislative authority, its enactments taking precedence over the remnants of feudal or canon law, its powers and responsibilities superseding those of the Church or municipalities, or indeed any other public agency. Its economic responsibilities were already assuming the shape appropriate to a unified nation state for it was increasingly expected to use its powers in the interest of the whole nation, and to respond in that spirit to the problems generated by a changing world economy—for example, to international competition, to fluctuations in domestic economic activity, to monetary instability, and to major shifts in the distribution of wealth between social classes. At the same time, of course, central government was expected to play its traditional role as defender of the independent nation state against foreign enemies and as the ultimate source of law and order at home.

Tudor and Stuart governments were thus perpetually in need of funds to support a rising level of political and economic activities.

Naturally enough it was the commercial and propertied classes that were most directly affected, for good or ill, by government interventions in the economic process and that were likely to find themselves funding (whether by loans or taxes) mounting government expenditures. Two things gave them the political self-confidence to oppose the economic paternalism of the early Stuarts and thus light a fuse for the English Revolution. The first was the sheer inefficiency of State intervention, which seemed to them to be hindering rather than advancing national economic progress. The second was the development of the Puritan work ethic, a religious ideology which glorified the individualistic pursuit of material wealth. Fundamental to English Puritan theology was the notion of a God-given calling or vocation through which each individual could pursue mutually consistent ethical and economic ends. Before the end of the seventeenth century the economic virtues of the acquisitive society—such as diligence, frugality, and rational calculation—were part of the conventional moral code of criteria for human behaviour in the market-place.

2

Political economy in the shadow of the scientific revolution

> Those who have handled sciences have been either men
> of experiment or men of dogmas. The men of experiment
> are like the ant, they only digest and use; the reasoners
> resemble spiders who make cobwebs out of their sub-
> stance. But the bee takes a middle course; it gathers the
> material from the flowers of the garden and of the field
> but transforms and digests it by a power of its own.
>
> Francis Bacon

Early in the seventeenth century a conflict of ideas on the nature, power, rights, and functions of the modern sovereign state combined with pressures set up by social discontent and economic uncertainty, by religious doubts and prejudices, and by those who were manipulating the contemporary power structure, to produce a crisis of expectations in relation to the English monarchy, a crisis which exploded into civil war and did not find a constitutional equilibrium until the 1690s. It was against this disturbed backcloth of political problems, events and upheavals, and within a new framework of religious, philosophical, and scientific ideas that seventeeth-century thinkers began to formulate rational explanations of the way the market economy worked, or ought to work.

By exacerbating the nation's economic problems and reducing the consistency and effectiveness of State censorship, the political upheavals injected an effervescent quality into the polemical literature focused on economic questions. A shifting, unpredictable, pattern of political and economic change is perhaps not the most fertile context for systematic thinking about the causes and consequences of alternative policies. What encouraged certain seventeenth-century writers to found their economic policy prescriptions on arguments that were not only imaginative but also disciplined was the example of the intellectual revolution that was currently taking shape in the natural sciences.

Most modern accounts of the scientific revolution of the seventeenth century focus mainly on its significance for the progress of ideas in the 'hard', natural sciences, which today's conventional academic curricula distinguish sharply from such studies as philosophy or history. It is important to notice, however, that these distinctions did not have the same significance in the intellectual environment of the seventeenth century, and that to the philosophers and scientists of that era 'science' meant knowledge in the broadest sense. The changes in scientific ideas had pervasive implications for people's perception of all aspects of their material and immaterial beliefs.

The profound changes—political, social, cultural, economic, and technological—taking shape in the sixteenth century had undermined the conventional structure of beliefs of the relation of man to God on the one hand and to the material world on the other, forcing the educated élite to reconsider the foundations of reliable knowledge. For a long time the main effect of the Renaissance and the Reformation was to harden the conservatism of the traditional centres of learning and research—the universities. In the belief that the truth about the world, in all its material and immaterial aspects, lay embedded in the ancient classical texts and the Bible, most fifteenth- and sixteenth-century academics had devoted themselves to correcting and reinterpreting their heritage of medieval translations and to searching the archives for lost originals. The printing press and the international use of Latin as the common language of scholarship stimulated scholars by facilitating rapid dissemination of new translations and commentaries through the leading European universities. But it was a research programme subject to disappointingly diminishing returns, containing little of interest to new generations of students feeling the need for a world-view consistent with the changes that had already transformed their religious, political, and socio-economic enviroment.

Among those who consciously set out to reconstruct the traditional system of ideas in which they had been brought up, and to justify a new approach to the advancement of knowledge, there were three diverse contemporaries, each of whom made a distinctive personal impact on ways of thinking in the seventeenth century and beyond, and who are generally assigned leading roles in any modern account of the scientific revolution: Francis Bacon (1561–1626), Galileo (1564–1642), and René Descartes (1596–1650). Each has a special claim to have set his mark on a new approach to scientific discovery—in the social as well as in the natural sciences.

In a sense, Galileo, the astronomer, may be said to have achieved the most spectacular breakthrough in transforming the world picture of the seventeenth-century educated élite, by popularizing a Copernican, heliocentric view of the universe. Certainly a vision of the universe in which the earth and its human inhabitants were no longer the central feature raised far-reaching religious and philosophical issues. Moreover, the fact that Roman Catholic officialdom dealt with these difficult issues by invoking the terror of the Inquisition turned an academic debate among astronomers (using mathematical arguments intelligible only to a few specialists) into a crusade for freedom of enquiry and against authoritarian dogma. Galileo's *Dialogue Concerning the Two Chief World-Systems, Ptolemaic and Copernican*, which put the case for the Copernican theory in the guise of an uncommitted statement of pros and cons, was already a best-seller before the Inquisition's ban took effect; and the author's forced recantation and long imprisonment brought him international fame and sympathy. The English poet John Milton, for example, was among those who visited him shortly before his death in 1638 (in a not very austere prison) and he wrote indignantly of 'the famous Galileo, grim, old, a prisoner to the Inquisition for thinking in Astronomy other than the Franciscan and Dominican licensors of thought'.

In effect, Galileo's contribution to the transition from medieval to modern science stemmed more from his approach, his research style, than from his result. For example, in opposing the Aristotelian view that knowledge is the 'grasping of essences', and in insisting that advances in knowledge hinge on the systematic application of mathematical techniques of analysis to experimental observations, he revealed himself as one of the earliest and clearest exponents of the research methodology that Newton was to develop so fruitfully. Similarly, in turning away from the traditional scholastic preoccupation with primary causes, and in reformulating key questions in terms of the *how* rather than the *why* of motion, Galileo opened wide windows on a new vision of the natural world as a self-contained, mathematically definable machine. It was a vision that, after being imaginatively elaborated by Descartes and Newton, served as an inspiration to the founder of English classical political economy, Adam Smith.

In assessing the impact of Galileo's research style on his own era, however, two things seem to emerge as crucial in accounting for his heroic stature. The first was his systematic rejection of the Aristotelian research tradition—especially the Aristotelian questions concerning the primary causes of motion. The second was his success in reaching unexpected but convincing results on empirical questions of major practical significance. The first factor struck a chord that was in tune with the spirit of the age in the history of ideas: the spirit of anti-authoritarianism. The second gave his distinctive research method credence among leading scientists and philosophers. True, nothing succeeds like success, but it was Galileo's unwillingness to be shackled by ancient dogma that enable him to take the lead in the scientific revolution of the seventeenth century and that was to assure him of the veneration of the giants even of twentieth-century science and philosophy such as Albert Einstein: 'the *leit-motiv* which I recognize in Galileo's work is the passionate fight against any kind of dogma based on authority. Only experience and careful reflection are accepted by him as criteria of truth.'[1]

Essentially the same anti-authoritarian ideology coloured the views of both Bacon and Descartes on the best way to advance human knowledge. Indeed it is hard to explain the charismatic quality of Bacon's influence on English scientists of the seventeenth century in any other terms. Without its ideological overtones it is hardly likely that practising scientists (in the modern sense of the term) could have swallowed so readily the methodological advice of a lawyer-politician without research experience, with no mathematics and with a weak grasp of the new ideas and experimental techniques that were illuminating the frontiers of early seventeenth-century natural science—for instance, the new astronomy, or Galileo's telescopic observations. What was so stimulating about Bacon's *Novum Organum* (so called to indicate his intention to supersede Aristotle's *Organon*) was a combination of three things. First and foremost there was its contempt for dogmatism and ritualism, its call for a new start: 'We must begin anew from the very foundations unless we revolve forever in a circle with mean and contemptible progress.' Second was his concept of a vast collaborative research programme in which the combined efforts of an army of seekers after truth—the ant-like fact-collectors, the spider-like theorists, and the bee-like analysts—would each contribute to a cumulative advancement of knowledge about the natural world. Third was his clear moral vision of the goals of the research enterprise, his conviction that the knowledge thus acquired would serve not only God (by decoding the divine book of nature) but also man, through its application to the betterment of his material conditions of life.

There was thus room in Bacon's philosophy for a variety of routes to a new world-view. His sense of being on the threshold of a new era of intellectual discovery and control over nature justified the innovators more effectively than his rhetorical onslaught on the 'degenerate learning' of the schoolmen 'shut up in the cells of a few authors (chiefly Aristotle their dictator) as their persons were shut up in the cells of monasteries and knowing little history, either of nature or time'. His conviction that the study of the book of nature is the key to an understanding of the will of God gave a religious flavour to his message that made it particularly congenial to the Puritan social ethic that gathered adherents through the seventeenth century: 'only let man regain his right over Nature which belongs to him by the gift of God; let there be given to him the power, right reason and sound religion will teach him how to apply it'. His emphasis on the unity of knowledge, on the prior importance of assembling and correlating a foundation of empirical evidence from every area, and on the potential contribution of each serious enquirer—whether scholar, craftsman, or statesman—had the effect of widening the scope of the intellectual community dedicated to the pursuit of disciplined learning.

Baconianism, which reached a peak of influence in the Restoration period, has generally been identified (then as later) with an obsessively inductive, essentially experimental methodology, and as being the chief inspiration for the co-operative, utilitarian research programme envisaged by the founders of the Royal Society. Not surprisingly, perhaps, the methodological prescriptions conventionally associated with Bacon's name have been more narrowly interpreted than is consonant either with the author's own intentions or with the actual practice of leading Baconian scientists. It is worth recalling, for example, that Bacon did not see the most productive scientist as being analogous either to the data-amassing ant or the theory-spinning spider of his parable, but as like the industrious bee, flitting purposefully from flower to flower and extracting nectar to be re-fashioned into a more precious substance altogether. In the end, it would seem that Bacon's most enduring and significant contribution to the scientific revolution was not a myopically inductive methodology, but a bold, open-minded, free-ranging attitude of enquiry. 'The universe', he wrote, 'should not be narrowed down to the limits of the understanding, as has been man's practice up till now, but rather the understanding must be stretched and enlarged to take in the image of the universe as it is discovered.' And when—with characteristic self-confidence—he assessed his own qualifications for pontificating on the advancement of learning, he listed them in the following terms: 'as having a mind nimble and versatile enough to catch the resemblances of things (which is the chief point), and at the same time steady enough to fix and distinguish their subtler differences; as being gifted by nature with the desire to seek, patience to doubt, fondness to meditate, slowness to assert, readiness to consider, carefulness to dispose and set in order; and as being a man that neither affects what is new nor admires what is old, and that hates every kind of imposture.' That was Bacon's image of the good scientist: it could be an equally valid description of a good economist.

The other member of the trio of early seventeenth-century intellectual giants whose reconstructions in the philosophy of science contributed significantly to the new world-view that emerged from the scientific revolution was René Descartes. Like Galileo and Bacon, he reacted openly against scholastic dogmatism and academic authority—though, paradoxically, not against the institutional authority of the Roman Catholic church. For when Galileo was disciplined by the Inquisition of 1633 for publishing a defence of Copernican theory, Descartes hastily withdrew from the printers a book of his own whose cosmology was based on heliocentric principles. More completely even than Bacon, Descartes was determined to replace Aristotle's outworn philosophy by a coherent system of thought of his own making, to start with a clean slate and to use only those ideas and theories which were either intuitively acceptable or rationally justifiable to himself. He began with two basic assumptions and a starting hypothesis—a belief in the existence of God as the primary first cause, a belief in himself as a thinking soul ('Je pense, donc je suis'), and the hypothesis of a divine rational order, reducible to a set of universal physical laws, underlying the workings of the material world.

Neither in their substance nor in their implications were these initial presumptions wholly remarkable for a seventeenth-century philosopher. What gave Descartes's research programme its most distinctive quality was his choice of mathematics as the crucial instrument of inquiry, the key to full understanding of the rationally explicable world order. For that offered the sceptical scientist a route to ultimate certainty—the most desirable of goals for an intellectual community disenchanted with the traditional doctrines of its centres of education and research. What he then set out to do was to develop a theoretical model consistent with his rational-order hypothesis, a model which was in principle definable and testable by rigorously mathematical techniques of analysis. Descartes was himself an innovator in this sphere, the inventor of an analytical and coordinate geometry, and one might have expected that his approach would rapidly have lost its appeal for the majority of students who were not themselves mathematically gifted. In the event, however, his vision of a universe organized on precise and predictable principles, a clock-work universe, was illuminated for seventeenth-century thinkers of all kinds by the analogy with the everyday instrument of a clock.

Typical of Descartes's expository technique, indeed, was his liberal use of similes and metaphors to reduce complex phenomena to clear simple terms, intelligible to any sensible individual who was willing to follow a rational argument. The concept of a mechanical system, analogous to a clock, provided a multi-purpose analytical framework within which to discuss a wide variety of natural phenomena in terms of the measurable movements, size and interconnections of their atomistic constituents. Given the sharp distinction he drew between the physical and animal features of the real world on the one hand, and its divine and spiritual aspects on the other, the clockwork symbolism and mathematical precision of his arguments lent an appearance of objectivity to his research method. It was an appearance particularly attractive to empirically-minded Baconians who were weary of the religious dissension and obscurantism that impeded the advance of knowledge about the natural world.

Descartes's new system of philosophy aroused interest and controversy in both Britain and France. For students such as John Locke, whose intellectual attitudes were formed in the 1640s and 1650s, Descartes's radical approach seemed to inject a breath of fresh air into the stuffy Aristotelian philosophy which was staple fare in the curricula of the leading universities. Even those who were hostile to the mechanical philosophy and revolted by the impersonality of its image of a clockwork universe were excited by the range and power of the rigorously rational arguments which represented the heart and core of Descartes's original contributions to physics, optics, mathematics, and general philosophy. The part of his message which had most attraction for the relatively pragmatic English thinkers was, first, his emphasis on the improvement of the quality of human life on earth as the chief goal of scientific investigation; secondly, the new insights promised by the application of quantitative techniques of analysis in a variety of areas which had hitherto seemed amenable only to qualitative arguments (political arithmetic is a good example); and thirdly, the new programmes of research opened up by the possibility of applying his atomistic, mechanical model to, say, biological and chemical studies, that is, to areas which had been largely subject to teleological and/or alchemical modes of explanation.

In spite of the evident differences in the nature of the contributions which Galileo the Italian astronomer, Bacon the English statesman, and Descartes the French philosopher made to the way seventeenth-century thinkers perceived their world and their prospects of understanding it, they had one important characteristic in common. What commended their messages so powerfully to their contemporaries was their rejection of bookish authority and their assertion of the potential of the observing, reasoning, and calculating human mind in grasping God's blueprint for the universe. For man's weakening faith in the certainty of salvation in the next world they exchanged an optimistic confidence in the progress of his knowledge of this.

At a time when the nation's scientists, philosophers, bankers, merchants, theologians, public officials, and their personal assistants belonged to an identifiable intellectual community, read the same books, and moved in the same social circles, those who addressed themselves to economic questions drew freely on the ideological and methodological doctrines of the new science. Merchants, businessmen, and estate owners consciously applied a Baconian methodology in basing their management decisions on quantitative assessments of their properties and incomes. Government officials were increasingly concerned to collect empirical evidence, particularly statistical data on economic matters, and habitually sought advice on the probable consequences of specific economic policies from a broad spectrum of scientists, philosophers, and other informed observers in the intellectual community. The writings of both Bacon and Descartes supported a growing consensus that the fruits of scientific investigation would be primarily economic and that technological discoveries relating to agriculture, navigation, manufacturing or mining, for example, would lead directly to improvements in the material conditions of life of human beings generally. Given this ideological context it was not surprising that the rational, calculating, empirical techniques of analysis which were generating exciting new research programmes in the natural sciences were applied to the study of society itself—especially since it was practising natural scientists who were among the first to think systematically about social science.

Among the seventeenth-century Englishmen who contributed significantly to the foundations for a systematic study of society, there were two who strikingly exemplified the scientific spirit of their age: Sir William Petty (1623–87) and John Locke (1632–1704). Both were Oxford-educated and became leading Fellows of the Royal Society; both were practising physicians; and both wrote substantial essays on economic analysis to justify policy prescriptions focused on urgent economic problems facing the governments of their day. Neither was ready to separate political from economic considerations, still less from their moral implications.

The scientist who most deliberately carried the Baconian methodology over to economics was Sir William Petty, a self-made man whose career provides a vivid illustration of the opportunities open to an ambitious and talented seventeenth-century intellectual in an age of social and political upheaval and scientific adventure. The son of a modestly affluent Hampshire clothier, Petty left school at 14 to join a coastal ship as cabin boy. When put ashore to mend a leg broken in an accident at sea, he seized the chance of entering the Jesuit College at Caen, in Normandy, in order to improve his school Latin, Greek, and French and also to acquire such rudiments of arithmetic and astronomy as might be useful to a practical seaman. On his return to England he joined the Royal Navy, where he served a short spell of duty before going abroad again in search of further education—mainly in Holland, where he took up medicine. Later, after royalist Oxford had succumbed to the parliamentary forces, he went up to Brasenose College to deepen his medical studies. There, he was so successful in impressing the progressive scientists of his day with his practical and theoretical skills that he was appointed Professor of Anatomy at the age of 27.

It was, however, in Ireland, to which he went in 1652, as physician to the army of occupation, that the young Oxford professor began to focus his attention on questions of economic policy. At that stage, the most pressing economic problem facing the conquerors of rebellious Ireland was how to organize an orderly distribution of forfeited lands to the soldiers and adventurers whose settlement was designed to consolidate the conquest. It was obvious that the first requirement was some kind of land survey, and Petty—who brought to his work the acquisitive values and intellectual energy of his Puritan middle-class heritage—persuaded the Commissioners charged with the survey to let him conduct an elaborate research project (aimed at establishing the dimensions of Ireland's human, agricultural, and industrial resources) in return for an advance of one penny for every three acres surveyed. He recruited a staff of about a thousand men (ranging from educated clerks and experienced surveyors to common soldiers who carried out the legwork), completed the survey in less than two years, and amassed a substantial personal fortune in cash and land.

The survey represented the first stage of a continuing research programme designed to assess Ireland's total economic resources. In the 1660s Petty used it as a basis for the first atlas of Ireland. In the 1670s he expanded it into a detailed economic survey entitled *The Political Anatomy of Ireland*, prefacing it with the following robust methodological statement:

Sir Francis Bacon, in his Advancement of Learning, hath made a judicious Parallel in many particulars, between the Body Natural and the Body Politick and between the Arts of preserving both in Health and strength. And it is as reasonable, that as Anatomy is the best foundation of one, so also of the other; and that to practice upon the Politick without knowing the Symmetry, Fabrick and Proportion of it, is as casual as the practice of Old-women and Empyricks. Now, because Anatomy is not only necessary in Physicians but laudable in every Philosophical person whatsoever, I therefore, who profess no Politicks, have, for my curiosity at large, attempted the first Essay of Political Anatomy.[2]

In effect, Petty was a forerunner of the modern breed of government economic adviser. His economic essays were addressed directly to policy makers (most were not published until after his death), and, in contrast to the majority of seventeenth-century pamphleteers writing on economic affairs, he set out to formulate and justify his policy prescriptions in terms of the national interest as a whole, rather than from the point of view of a particular section or class of society. More important still, he based his economic analyses on a new kind of empirical research, familiar enough in style to seventeenth-century scientists investigating the natural world, but never before applied systematically to the social sphere. What Petty and his followers called 'political arithmetic' and defined as 'the art of reasoning upon things related to government' was an economic research programme which represented the beginnings of an objective discipline of applied economics.

Petty's research was not of course confined to Ireland. Already in 1662, the year in which he was experimenting with the first prototype of his invention for a double bottom boat, he had written *A Treatise of Taxes and Contributions*, containing a miscellany of sharp observations, incisive economic analysis, and detailed policy advice on contemporary questions of public finance. Throughout this early pamphlet runs the theme that was to recur in all Petty's later economic writings: the importance of founding public economic policies on a basis of systematically compiled data and informed quantitative estimates of the nation's human and material resources. During the 1665-7 war with Holland he wrote *Verbum Sapienti*, a pamphlet on the practical problems of financing the national war effort in which he attempted the first estimates of national income and wealth for England and Wales. In the 1670s he developed his favourite themes in what became his best-known work, *Political Arithmetick*, written to rebut those commentators who were lamenting the nation's economic decline. The preface to that work contained his own description of his distinctive research style: 'The method I take to do this is not very usual; for instead of using only Comparative and superlative Words and Intellectual Arguments, I have taken the course (as a Specimen of the Political Arithmetick I have long aimed at) to express myself in terms of *Number*, *Weight* or *Measure*; to use only Arguments of Sense and to consider only such Causes as have visible Foundations in Nature, leaving those that depend on the Mutable Minds, Opinions, Appetites and Passions of particular men, to the Consideration of others.'[3]

The lasting interest of Petty's 'method of political arithmetic' lies not in the quantitative estimates he generated—some of his followers (notably Gregory King) produced more careful and reliable national income estimates, for example—but in the analytical uses to which he put his numberings. His policy advice was supported by a logical reasoning process within a framework of theoretical concepts which he did not invent but which he defined and deployed consistently and imaginatively. It was predicated, moreover, upon a view of the economic role of the State which was as significant as his quantitative style of economic reasoning. Petty saw little scope for policy measure designed to influence directly the trend or pattern of economic events. For example, after admitting in the preface to his *Treatise*: 'I would now advertise the world that I do not think I can mend it . . . and that (say what I will or can) *things will have their course*' (italics supplied), he went on to condemn the manipulation of the currency as a 'breach of Publick Faith' and then, in a chapter on usury, referred to 'the variety and fruitlessness of making Civil Positive Laws against the Laws of Nature'.

On the other hand, Petty's enumeration in the *Treatise* of the proper avenues of public expenditure implied broad social responsibilities for government and raised issues which are still of crucial importance in twentieth-century economic debates. In particular, for example, he argued that there was an *economic* case (as well as a just case) for generous treatment not only of the helpless poor (the foundlings and the disabled) but also of the able-bodied unemployed. Indeed, after pointing out that '. . . it is unjust to let any starve when we think it just to limit the wages of the poor so that they can lay up nothing against their time of impotency and want of work', he went so far as to argue that it could be in the national interest to spend public funds in putting the unemployed to unproductive work: 'Now as to the work of these supernumeraries, let it be without expense of Foreign Commodities, and then it is no matter if it be employed to build a useless Pyramid upon Salisbury Plain, bring the Stones at Stonehenge to Tower Hill or the like; for at worst this would keep their minds to discipline and obedience and their bodies to a patience of more profitable labours when need shall require it.'[4]

There is a curiously modern ring to some of these phrases, which may seem at first glance to foreshadow twentieth-century debates on measures to alleviate unemployment—for example, J. M. Keynes's advocacy of pyramid building or of digging unnecessary holes in the ground as ways of increasing not only employment but also the real national product. These are superficial similarities, however. The fact is that Petty was following an ancient tradition of economic discourse rather than anticipating a modern macro-economic perspective. What seventeenth-century economic advisers typically addressed themselves to were the practical problems of the nation-state, and these were seen as analogous to the practical problems of managing a household. Petty dedicated his *Political Arithmetic* to the king because it was the royal domain he was endeavouring to assess and its management problems that the quantification was designed to inform.

In the event, Petty's aggregative approach to analysing and quantifying the nation's resources fell out of favour among English eighteenth-century theorists as the abstract notion of a self-equilibrating system gradually began to take precedence over the essentially political concept of the royal domain as the central object of economic analysis. Adam Smith, for example, was to announce that he had 'no great faith in political arithmetic' and it was not until the 1930s, when Keynes's macro-economic theorizing revolutionized the discipline, that we find leading economists again focusing on aggregative economic analysis. Nevertheless, Petty had broken new ground in basing his analyses of national economic problems on calculations of measurable economic magnitudes, on whose quantitative interrelationships the nation's productive power and taxable capacity evidently hinged. A long, if sporadic, stream of national income estimates compiled by diligent political arithmeticians following in his footsteps were produced over the next two and a half centuries. At the same time, a distinguished tradition of administrative statistics (beginning with the overseas trade returns started at the end of the seventeenth-century) enabled British parliamentarians and civil servants and their critics to examine contemporary economic policy options in the light of objective quantitative evidence on the way the economic system operated in practice.

For John Locke, too, the policy problems that later generations were to call economic were indistinguishable from the general problems of government, and most of his writings had more political than economic content. It was as a political philosopher, and to some extent as an epistemologist, that Locke made his most powerful impact on the development of ideas. With the exception of the *Essay on Human Understanding* most of his works remained unpublished during his lifetime. Evidently Locke had more reason than Petty to fear the consequences of being identified as the author of controversial opinions for he could not claim, as Petty did, to be without political affiliations.

The son of a captain in Cromwell's parliamentary army, Locke left Oxford in 1667 to enter the household of a Whig politican, Lord Ashley, Earl of Shaftesbury, who was to disgrace himself under the Restoration monarchy by actively plotting to exclude the Catholic James, Duke of York, from the throne. Locke's association with the conspiracy (which collapsed with the Monmouth rebellion), his openly Whiggish politics, his anti-authoritarian philosophy, and his reasoned opposition to arbitrary or absolutist government did not endear him to the Stuart monarchy and effectively excluded him from public office from 1673 to 1689. Indeed, for the last six years of that period he remained in voluntary exile in Holland, returning only after the constitutional monarchy of William and Mary was established in England. Even under that regime, the theory of popular sovereignty outlined in his two treatises on government was too radical to be palatable to authority, and he dared not acknowledge authorship.

So although Locke was personally associated with some of the principal actors in the seventeenth-century revolution in economic ideas, and though he won international acclaim when his *Essay on Human Understanding*—to which he was proud to put his name—appeared (in England in 1690 and in French translation in 1700), the posthumous impact of his writings was more stimulating than they had ever been in his lifetime. Leibniz, for example, the German statesman, scientist, and professor of ethics, was sufficiently excited by the *Essay* to publish a critical dialogue entitled *New Essays on Human Understanding*, which appeared the year Locke died and in which an imaginary empiricist (whose arguments were largely lifted from Locke) debated with a rationalist representing Leibniz's own epistemological stance. Later still, Voltaire is reputed to have learned English in order to read Locke in the original, and the message which eighteenth-century writers drew from Locke's writings became heavily imbued with the spirit of a later age than his own, making it sometimes hard to distinguish the impact of Locke's own message from that of the Lockean theories which his admirers attributed to him.

The essence of the new science that emerged from the scientific revolution was a new way of perceiving the natural world and a set of techniques for finding out how it operated. Locke's friends, Boyle and Newton, had been among those who demonstrated the power of the new methods in advancing the frontiers of knowledge in the natural sciences. Locke's *Essay* was an attempt to extend their analytical-empirical approach to a study of the social world and to design a theory of knowledge which could rise above the disorderly civil and religious conflict of opinions that had so destabilized European society in the seventeenth century. It sought a scientifically impartial route to an understanding of the socially divisive issues of the day.

Starting from the religious position that man is a rational being who enjoys a special relationship with his rational Creator, Locke insisted that the human mind was inherently better equipped to achieve an intelligent understanding of the nature of man's relations with his fellows and with God than to understand the natural world in all its essentials. Following both Bacon and Descartes in accepting a 'blank sheet' conception of the enquiring human mind, Locke argued that educated individuals could work out for themselves the kind of moral and political behaviour appropriate to a rationally-ordered universe, provided that they were willing to deploy their God-given powers of observation and reasoning to decode the divine plan. The key assumption of Locke's theory of knowledge was that the moral and political laws according to which individuals *ought* to behave, and society *ought* to be organized, were analogous to the laws of nature that determined the operations of the physical universe. Thus, at a very early stage in the articulation of the rules of social behaviour in the modern capitalist economy—before the philosophers had begun to think of the economy as conceptually distinct from the polity—the 'whys' of specific economic policies began to determine the theories and concepts developed to explain *how* the economy operated naturally.

Locke's optimistically commonsensical approach to the human sciences of morals and politics was particularly attractive to an age which urgently needed to develop criteria governing the role of the state in maintaining political (including economic) order. No seventeenth-century writer on economic questions would have detached them from their moral dimensions. Most were agreed that the first requirement of a successful economic policy was that it should conform to acceptable principles of justice. This criterion was frequently invoked by Petty in his discussion of government taxation and expenditure policies. It was the starting point for the theory of property which Locke developed in his *Two Treatises on Civil Government*.[5] 'Justice', he wrote, 'gives to every Man a Title to the product of his honest Industry'; and he proceeded to envisage a 'state of nature', a conjectural stage in human history, when—given that the Divine Plan guaranteed ample natural resources to meet essential human needs and that each labourer had a duty to appropriate as much of those resources as he could use productively—the limits to an unequal distribution of property were set by the fact that all goods necessary to life were perishable. In that hypothetical golden age, government intervention was superfluous, for each labourer had an undisputed right to the property he created by his own surplus and no one's surplus would subtract from anyone else's means of subsistence. Only when the introduction of money—'some lasting thing which Men might keep without spoiling, and by mutual consent Men would take in exchange for the truly useful but perishable Support of Life'—made it possible for individuals to acquire more property than they could use creatively (or had themselves produced) was civil government needed to regulate the situation and adjudicate between unequal claims on natural resources in the interests of society as a whole: 'the end of Government itself . . . is the publick good and the preservation of Property.' Locke thus harnessed to a common framework what were (and still are) two of the most important and fundamental issues in political economy: the role of the State and the role of money.

It is important to notice that Locke defined the concepts of labour and capital more broadly than most economists have done. By labour he meant all kinds of productive activity—including entrepreneurial or capitalistic or professional activities as well as hired labour. In these broad terms it was the source of all wealth and it represented the individual's religious duty. Property covered an amorphous range of material and immaterial possessions—'lives, liberties and estates which I call by the general name of property'—and was not synonymous with private property or land. By narrowing Locke's definitions to accord with modern meanings of key words, later generations of political economists have succeeded in converting his arguments into a justification for private ownership of the means of production (and for the associated inequalities in the distribution of wealth). There is, however, no evidence that Locke himself saw his theory as a justification for a system of possessive individualism or for a profit-maximizing capitalist economy. On the contrary, his theory of property was a political rather than an economic theory and he explained the prevailing system of property distribution not in terms of 'natural rights', but of the social contract which he assumed to be implicit in the acceptance of a system of civil government: 'It is plain that the consent of Men have agreed to disproportionate and unequal Possessions of the Earth, I mean out of Society and Compact; for in Governments the Laws regulate it.'

Central to John Locke's political philosophy was the conviction that a rational society (which he equated to a harmonious, moral society) hinged on the mutual trust of its members. This system of trust formed the basis of the implicit social contract which he invoked to legitimate the legal and political discipline accepted by a society of free and equal individuals; and it was this same notion of an implicit contract, a pledge, which he used to explain the origin of money as stemming from the agreement of buyers and sellers to accept certain durable commodities, such as silver or gold, as standards of value in market exchange. The role of government was to ensure that the rules of the game embodied

in the freely accepted social contract were respected and
enforced. As far as monetary policy was concerned, it meant that
the prime criterion for government intervention in the monetary
system was maintenance of the market's confidence in the standard of value. To debase the currency—as governments had frequently been tempted to do in order to finance their military
ventures—was to perpetrate a fraud, which was the more heinous
because, according to Locke, 'the publick authority is the guarantee for the performance of all legal contracts'. Sir William
Petty had taken a similar moral stance in his *Treatise of Taxes
and Contributions*; for example, he described the practice of
debasement as 'a very pittiful and unequal way of Taxing the
people' and as a 'breach of Public Faith such as calling a thing
what it really is not'.

The problem confronting the monetary authorities in the
1690s, however, was the more insidious one of a deteriorating
silver coinage subject to continuous clipping. New issues from
the Mint had been milled at the edges from 1663 onwards, but
since the old clipped coins had never been withdrawn (and were
still at risk of further clipping) the majority of silver coins in
circulation belied their face values. By the early 1690s the disappearance of full weight coin into hoards, or to finance an
adverse trade balance was creating a shortage of currency at
the same time as the wartime inflation was driving up prices. It
was obvious that the authorities would need to take action to
regain control over the coinage and a spate of pamphlets and
reports showered the new government with advice on how it
should be done.

The recoinage controversy of the 1690s represented the first
sustained debate in the history of political economy, for the
options were wide open and in the process of justifying their
various prescriptions the protagonists generated a substantial
volume of economic analysis. The authorities could *either* accept
the current market situation and reduce the nominal weight of
coins to something near their actual average silver content
(contemporaries described this as 'raising the value of money',
modern economists would call it devaluation of the currency); *or*
recall the depreciated coin and replace it with full weight coin at

the standard nominal value; *or* take some intermediate course between a full devaluation and a full restoration.

What gives the controversy a special interest in the history of economic thought was, first of all, the intellectual distinction of the leading contributors to the debate. They included, beside John Locke, Sir John Houblon (Governor of the Bank of England), William Lowndes (Secretary of the Treasury), Thomas Neale (Master of the Mint from 1686 to 1699), Sir Isaac Newton (the next Master of the Mint), Sir Christopher Wren, and sundry well-known writers on economic matters generally, such as Sir Josiah Child, Nicholas Barbon, John Houghton and Charles Davenant. The second remarkable feature of this episode was the rationale for the solution that was accepted in practice—Locke's proposal that the English silver coinage should be restored to the nominal weights standardized at the time of Elizabeth I, which amounted to a full restoration.

The hard core of Locke's argument was his assumption that the intrinsic value of silver was fixed by common consent and ought to be guaranteed for all time by public authority. To change the standard would be to defraud those transactors who had accepted it as legally binding and so to destroy the confidence of the trading community in the market system, for 'men are absolved from the performance of their legal contracts if the quantity of silver under settled and legal denominations be altered'. In view of the fact that this was the most expensive solution mooted, it is on the face of it surprising that it proved the most acceptable to the political authorities. Lowndes, the Secretary to the Treasury, had written a clear, practical, and pragmatic report advocating, in effect, a 20 per cent devaluation, which would have recognized part, but not all, of the depreciation already effective in the market. Later generations of economists have tended to dismiss Locke's arguments for restoring the silver standard as being unsophisticated. It is true that he did not develop his economic analysis far enough to identify the gainers and losers from the so-called fraud involved in a devaluation; nor did he recognize that his solution would exacerbate the currency shortage problem and have deflationary effects on both prices and the level of activity. Nevertheless, by abstracting from the delicate question of market confidence, and from the moral criteria which Locke's contemporaries habitually applied to acts of monetary policy, modern economists tend to overlook considerations which were not (and still are not) irrelevant to the behaviour of economic decision-takers—however difficult they may be to integrate into a coherent explanatory or predictive theory. Whether Lowndes' prescription for a 20 per cent devaluation would have introduced more or less 'confusion' into the money market than the staged implementation of Locke's proposal, which was put into effect in 1696–9 remains an open question. What is interesting is that the essentially non-economic arguments favouring a return to the traditional fixed standard found political favour in 1695—as they were to do again during the Bullion controversy of the Napoleonic War period, and in the aftermath of the First World War.

The other monetary policy issue which stimulated a measure of economic analysis in the second half of the seventeenth century, and came to a head in the 1690s, revolved around the question of what was the desirable level of interest rates, and whether government could—or should—manipulate the actual level. The ideas and arguments developed in relation to these questions involved a somewhat broader range of economic analysis than the recoinage controversy, for they went further into considerations of the relations between real and monetary markets.

The practice of usury still carried a certain aura of sinfulness, in spite of the pervasiveness of the Puritan ethic, and government took responsibility for fixing a legal maximum rate of interest, a rate which had actually been brought down substantially in the course of the seventeenth century—from 10 per cent to 8 per cent in 1624 and then to 6 per cent in 1651. A number of writers in the Restoration period expressed doubts concerning the effectiveness and enforceability of the usury laws. Petty, for example, referred more than once to the 'vanity and fruitlessness of making Civil Positive Laws against the Laws of Nature'. At the same time, however, it became increasingly common for commentators seeking explanations for the enviable economic success of the Dutch to associate their expanding foreign trade and relatively high income levels with their relatively low interest rates. The question rose to the top of the economic debates of the 1690s following publication of a new edition of Sir Josiah Child's *Discourse about Trade*, which asserted that a low rate of interest was the chief cause of Dutch prosperity and advocated a lowering of the English legal maximum from 6 per cent to 4 per cent. This stimulated John Locke to refurbish an earlier paper of his own and to publish it under the title *Some Consequences of the Lowering of Interest and Raising the Value of Money* (1692).[6]

As so often in economic debates on the relation between the markets for money and the markets for things, the divergence of view hinged largely on implicit assumptions concerning the direction of causation. The empirical evidence suggested strongly that there was a connection between sustained economic prosperity and low interest rates. But whereas Child, for example, saw prosperity as caused by low interest rates, Locke argued that a relatively low rate of interest was the consequence of a relatively high level of incomes. He justified this in terms of a theory of the 'natural' rate of interest (which he defined as 'the price of the hire of money') and explained in simple supply and demand terms. For a country with a relatively ample supply of loanable funds, therefore, the rate of interest would 'naturally' be relatively low. More important still, his analysis led him to conclude that attempts to increase national wealth by compulsorily lowering interest rates would—in so far as they were effective—reduce the incentive of lenders to lend: 'and so the reducing of money to four per cent which will discourage men from lending will be a loss to the kingdom, in stopping so much of the current of money, which turns the wheels of trade.' Like Petty, however, he had doubts about the possibility of enforcing a legal maximum that was out of line with the 'natural' rate of interest: 'For since it is impossible to make a law that shall hinder a man from giving away his money or estate to whom he pleases, it will be impossible by any contrivance of law, to hinder men, skilled in the power they have, over their own goods, and the ways of conveying them to others, to purchase money to be lent to them at what rate soever their occasions shall make it necessary for them to have it.'

On these and other matters, then, the writers who wrote authoritatively on economic policy issues in the late seventeenth century offered their advice to governments in a self-consciously impartial spirit. They saw themselves as seekers after objective truth concerning the social sector of a divinely ordered universe, they defended their solutions to current policy problems in terms of the national interest, broadly conceived, and they saw no reason to detach the moral considerations relevant to human behaviour in the market-place from the more narrowly economic considerations such as self-interest, or market expansion, or high employment, or the supply of money. So when John Locke listed the consequences of a lowering of the legal maximum rate of interest he included not only the monetary consequences or the redistribution effects (away from widows and orphans and towards bankers and scriveners), but also the moral implications—'that it is likely to cause a great perjury in the nation'.

Historians of economic thought who have tried to distil the economic content of such arguments and to evaluate their contributions to later economic theories have found seventeenth-century analyses unsatisfactory and fragmentary largely for three reasons: first, because of their narrow focus on the specific policy issues which inspired them; secondly, because even where they used the concepts or terms with which modern economists operate they did not mean the same things by them; and thirdly, because their economic analyses were not designed to be read apart from their political and moral context. It was not until the eighteenth century that an identifiable 'science' of political economy began to take shape.

3

The search for scientific principles

Nature and Nature's laws lay hid in night
God said 'Let Newton be' and all was light.

Alexander Pope

The eighteenth century is often paraded in the history of ideas as the Age of Enlightenment. For the most significant legacy of the scientific revolution was not the theoretical or factual content of the new world-view, the new paradigm it established for natural science: it was the boundless horizons it opened up for human understanding generally. The European intellectual community thus inherited an unprecedented confidence in modern man's ability to unlock the secrets of God's blueprint for the universe, simply by applying his powers of observation and reasoning to an objective study of the world around him—the social world as well as the natural world.

The scientist who more than any other was responsible for the intellectual self-confidence of eighteenth-century thinkers was Isaac Newton. His rigorous, mathematically formulated inductions from empirical evidence had given the seal of certainty to the laws of motion discovered by Galileo and Descartes, revealed the elegant simplicity and order inherent in the 'most beautiful system of sun, planets and comets', and provided teleological justification for believing in the existence of a wise, all-powerful, interventionist God. By giving a unified explanation of events in the heavens and on earth—by showing, for example, that the movements of the heavenly bodies and the earthly tides were predictable in terms of the single principle of universal gravity—he caught the imagination not only of natural philosophers and technologists, but also of moral philosophers and politicians and theologians. It was not difficult to believe that a similar divinely regulated order must (or ought to) prevail in human relations as in the heavens and that adopting the Newtonian experimental, inductive method of inquiry—to the extent even of identifying metaphysical analogies to the powerful physical concept of gravity—would provide social philosophers with the key to God's plan for the moral and political world.

Most of the late seventeenth- or early eighteenth-century thinkers who set out to analyse social and political issues in a self-consciously scientific spirit emphasized their impartiality or objectivity, their readiness to submit their findings to informed criticism, and their deep respect for positive factual evidence. These were the recognized trademarks of the Royal Society scientist. They contrasted with the continental Cartesian approach, which assumed that the Divine Architect had already programmed into the human mind the innate ideas and the infallible reasoning powers that would guide the rational thinker to certain truth. The Newtonian style of scientific investigation had ideological implications which sychronized well with the pragmatic English epistemological tradition. It reflected a world-view based on Christian rather than deist preconceptions, and the early debates—for example, with Leibniz, a product of the Cartesian tradition—were exacerbated by their religious overtones. Leibniz, in an open letter to the Princess of Wales, accused both Locke and Newton of being irreligious, an accusation which was deliberately designed to discredit the English approach: 'Sir Isaac Newton and his followers', he wrote scornfully 'have also a very odd opinion concerning the Work of God. According to their Doctrine, God Almighty wants to wind up his Watch from Time to Time: otherwise it would cease to move. He had not it seems, sufficient Foresight to make it a perpetual Motion.'

As it turned out, the Cartesian view of God as the infinitely far-seeing Creator of a clockwork universe was more inimical to traditional religion than Newton's faithful vision of a law-governed universe kept in order by the watchful law-maker. He saw no need, for example, to define an ultimate cause for his universal principle of gravity, being content to infer its existence from the cosmic facts it could be used to explain: '. . . to us it is enough that gravity does really exist, and acts according to the laws which we have explained, and abundantly serves to account for all the motions of the celestial bodies and of our sea.' For the Cartesians, by contrast, once God had fulfilled his original function as the 'author of nature' his work was done, and when eighteenth-century astronomers discovered that the solar system was self-regulating and cyclic it became easy to eliminate the deity from natural science altogether.

Identification of an analogy between a self-regulating solar system and a self-regulating economy had to wait until the philosophers spinning theories to explain or predict human behaviour in the market-place learned to separate the concept of an economic system—an economy in the modern sense of that term—from the polity in which the contemporary economic problems arose. Meanwhile, growth in the scale and complexity of commerce and industry and the associated extension of its international and national dimensions stimulated a swelling stream of writings on questions of political economy. Most of them were written with the object of prescribing for or against specific forms of legislative intervention in the markets for money or goods or labour. To an increasing extent they sought to justify their prescriptions on scientific lines, in terms of self-evident 'natural laws' which the Divine Legislator was presumed to have laid down to maintain order in civil society and which were analogous to the physical laws now the subject of consensus among scientists investigating the material world. What they were searching for, in effect, were the economic laws and regularities which evidently co-ordinated the activities of a multitude of individuals operating in the overlapping markets for money, goods, and labour. Already many writers dealing with economic questions had begun to argue in terms of impersonal forces which tended to stimulate and then stabilize economic change, and which they associated with the political problems of reconciling economic conflicts between personal self-interest and the public interest. The assumption of a naturally self-equilibrating mechanism inherent in all free markets was in tune with the anti-authoritarian political attitudes current in post-Revolution England; and the concepts of balance and equilibrium, and of self-reversing flows in channels of circulation, became increasingly familiar in discussions of international trade and payments, or price formation, and of the circulation of money.

The problem situation faced by most commentators on economic policy issues in the early eighteenth century bears a striking resemblance to the preoccupations of economists in the late twentieth century. Unemployment was seen as the prime political problem, for it was relevant *both* to the maintenance of national economic activity *and* to a stable social order, which was evidently at risk when the distribution of incomes between rich and poor shifted in unacceptable directions. Seventeenth-century observers (Locke, for example) had already articulated a relation between the amount of money in circulation, on the one hand, and both the levels of commodity prices and interest rates, or the volume of trade and employment, on the other. What Locke had failed to explain was the mechanism of interaction between these variables. According to Richard Cantillon, for example, writing in the early 1730s: 'Mr Locke has clearly seen that the abundance of money makes everything dear, but he has not considered how it does so.' What was required, as Cantillon saw, was to map the probable routes by which changes in the supply of (or demand for) money worked through the real and financial processes of markets to affect the aggregate levels of prices, output, and employment. Accordingly, like J. M. Keynes two centuries later, Cantillon set out to develop a general theory of employment, interest, and money—a macro-economic theory which should explain the interdependence of real and financial transactions in a free capitalist economy. The need for a systematic theory of money and economic activity had been dramatically demonstrated earlier in the century when John Law, a speculator and financier, gave advice on monetary policy to the French government, with results that were at first brilliantly successful but which ended in financial disaster.

One of the most interesting features of the intellectual community which laid the foundations for a distinct discipline of political economy was its cosmopolitan quality. The early English economists were often equally at home in the British Isles and in Western Europe, some of them wrote in French as readily as in English, and their theories were informed by intelligent direct observation of economic events and institutions in the developing economies of England, Scotland, Holland, and France. More important still in shaping the economic prescriptions of some of them was that they were offering advice to economic policy makers operating in systems that were a great deal more dirigiste and authoritarian in ideology and political structure than the system which emerged from the English Revolution of 1688. John Law, Richard Cantillon, and Sir James Steuart are three contrasting cases in point.

John Law, for example, the son of an Edinburgh goldsmith, began to take an interest in questions of money and banking in the post-Revolution debates of the 1690s which led to the foundation of the Banks of England and of Scotland, as well as to the English recoinage of 1696–9. Unfortunately, the misadventure of a duel in 1694—he killed his opponent and bolted from the English prison where he was awaiting trial in 1695—forced Law to take refuge on the Continent. During a brief return to his Scottish estates in the early 1700s he wrote his major tract on economics, *Money and Trade considered with a Proposal for Supplying the Nation with Money*, which he published anonymously in 1705. The impending union between Scotland and England drove the gaol-breaker abroad again and not until after he had won international fame and fortune as Comptroller-General to the French government did Law get a royal pardon from George I and the freedom of the City of Edinburgh.

Law's major contribution to the development of economic thinking came less from his published analysis than from the consequences of his extraordinary success in persuading the French Regent to adopt what contemporaries called his System. The essence of Law's System—the main arguments for which were deployed in *Money Considered*, written when he was offering advice to the Scottish government—was to replace conventional metallic money by a managed paper currency (issued by a central bank and guaranteed by central government). The object of the System he expounded to the French government was to expand the money supply on a scale sufficient to stimulate an economic boom in France, fuelled by the natural resources available in its huge North American colony of Louisiana.

What Law grasped more clearly than most of his contemporaries were two things: first, that in an economy suffering from unemployed labour resources, an expansion in the supply of money could set off a virtuous circle of prosperity by increasing consumer demand, advancing to producers the investible funds they needed to raise output faster than domestic consumption or prices, so generating extra exports and ensuring a favourable (or at any rate avoiding an unfavourable) balance of trade; Locke and Petty among others had noted that a higher level of economic activity was associated with a larger supply of money; Law injected a dynamic into this equation by arguing that, since 'the increase of most goods depends on the demand', an increase in the supply of money would stimulate an increase in the level of employment. Secondly, that the value of money depends crucially on the *confidence* of those using it to exchange it for commodities and that a paper currency which could, in principle, be expanded or contracted in strict relation to the credit-worthy demand for it was less likely to provoke disturbing fluctuations in prices and in employment than a purely metallic currency, the supply of which depended on the balance of trade or the output of mines.

Confidence, however, is a more volatile variable than simple economic logic can account for and is easily shaken—either by the ineptitude (real or imagined) of those who implement economic policy, or by unexpected economic events. The cardinal error of Law's System was that it was based on a theory which grossly oversimplified the role of money, treating it as no more than an exchange token. 'Money' he asserted , 'is not the value *for* which goods are exchanged but the value *by* which they are exchanged'; and in his determination to provide buyers and sellers with a currency which they would never have any temptation to hoard, he ignored the store-of-value function which gold or silver coin served so effectively.

In the event, the spectacular financial crisis which destroyed Law's System in 1720 was due as much to errors of political judgement as to his failure to appreciate the full complexity of the interrelationships between money and credit in a developing market economy. Law had been heavily promoting his scheme for a note-issuing central bank to European governments (beginning with Scotland in 1704) for more than a decade, when the death of Louis XIV eventually paved the way for him to gain a favourable hearing in an almost bankrupt France. In 1716 he persuaded the Regent to approve the establishment of a *Banque Générale*, the first French note-issuing joint stock bank, and then, late in 1717, of the *Compagnie d'Occident*, a chartered company enjoying a monopoly of trade with, and complete administrative control over, the French colony of Louisiana, a territory stretching from the Gulf of Mexico to Canada.

As director-in-chief of these two initially very successful enterprises Law enjoyed great economic power in France and a brilliant international reputation as a financial wizard. By royal edict (on Law's advice) all taxes were to be remitted to the Exchequer in notes of the *Banque Générale*, while the *Compagnie d'Occident* went on to swallow up the other French trading companies in Africa and the Indies (being then renamed the *Compagnie des Indes*), took over a substantial chunk of the government's floating debt, and managed the collection of the royal revenues. The fact that this was an era of great optimism concerning the development potential of the New World (in Britain the contemporaneous stock market boom culminated in the bursting of the South Sea Bubble in 1720) helped to ensure that Law's imaginative schemes to restore the finances of the French monarchy, by raising the level of activity in the depressed French economy, would attract massive financial support from private investors. Nor did the System remain a financial dream. There was a lively French building boom, unemployment was drastically reduced, and the population of Louisiana rose tenfold. In January 1720 (shortly after becoming a naturalized French citizen and a Roman Catholic), John Law was appointed Comptroller-Générale of Finance to the French monarchy.

There was of course a price to be paid in the form of accelerating inflation; and the stock market mania associated with the speculative building bonanza (during which the shares of Law's *Compagnie des Indes* rose fiftyfold in two years) was bound to end in a sharp fall—in 1720 as much as in the New York stock market crash of 1929, say. What Law's experiment demonstrated, however, was not merely the inevitable reversal implicit in an excessive stock market boom, but that the market's confidence in the value of a government-guaranteed paper money was only as strong as its confidence in the government's readiness to honour the rules of the game it had chosen to lay down. He should have listened to the merchants of Lyons who, when objecting to the transformation of the *Banque Générale* into a *Banque Royale* (which Law achieved in 1719), wrote: 'The mere name of the king arouses distrust. His majesty it is true . . . is master by force in his kingdom, but as to confidence and credit, these he cannot create, however great his authority, except in the way individuals do in order to maintain their credit, that is by paying.' Instead, Law helped to drive up the price of his Mississippi stock by printing bank notes which he then lent to new subscribers. Then, when the unbridled rise in note circulation set off the inevitable flight from paper into coin, one of his first acts as French Comptroller-Générale was to get a royal edict issued prohibiting private individuals from holding gold or silver of more than 500 livres in total. It was soon painfully evident that confidence in the money market could not be enforced by royal decree, and within a very few months the owners of both the notes and the stock that had been the insubstantial building blocks of Law's System were engaged in a headlong rush to convert them into goods, or land, or gold, or silver—indeed into anything whose value might be expected to have some durability.

The spectacular failure of the System, bringing down with it the *Banque Royale* as well as the chartered company with which it had been merged, proved an object lesson to eighteenth-century policy makers and writers on economic affairs, in Britain as well as in France. The lesson most contemporary observers derived from it was that only a metallic currency could command enough confidence to be viable. So although some writers (such as Bishop Berkeley or David Hume) recognized that the level of economic activity in an under-employed economy might be lifted by expanding the money supply, Law's experiment had effectively discredited all plans for a managed paper currency. Henceforth most monetary theorists preferred to define money exclusively in terms of the precious metals, and to ignore the role of money-substitutes in adding to effective demand.

Richard Cantillon, who had lived in France and actively specu-lated through the era of Law's System (cannily unloading his

Mississippi stock in time to make a profit), was particularly perceptive in his description of the contrasting experience of the Bank of England, which had successfully extricated itself from the contemporaneous South Sea Bubble: 'The Bank opened a subscription engaging trusty and solvent people to join as guarantors of large amounts to maintain the credit and circulation of the Bank-notes. It was by this last refinement that the credit of the Bank was maintained in 1720 when the South Sea Bubble collapsed. As soon as it was publicly known that the subscription list was filled by wealthy and powerful people, the run on the Bank ceased and deposits were brought in as usual.'[1] In short, the crucial difference which he identified between the Bank of England and the *Banque Royale* was that the former was a private corporation, working within a familiar financial framework and managing its affairs according to accepted commercial principles. True, it was the government's bank and played an important part in the management of the National Debt, but it was relatively free from government intervention in its credit policies; indeed it was its private backers who steadied the nerves of the mass of its depositors in times of crisis.

John Law had a bee in his bonnet, a panacea in his pocket, and his writings, or his advice to governments, were dominated by a passion to persuade the authorities to adopt his prescription for raising the level of economic activity by manipulating the money supply. Richard Cantillon and Sir James Steuart shared his concern for making the fullest possible use of national resources as the prime economic policy objective. They too lived and wrote in a European continental context where absolute monarchies were the norm and government intervention in economic affairs was typically more acceptable than was the case in eighteenth-century Britain. They differed from Law, however, in that their writings were inspired more by an essentially scientific interest in understanding the way the market economy worked than by a desire to promote highly specific economic policy proposals. They read widely and critically in the literature of economic affairs, analysed their own direct observations, and deliberately set out to identify the kind of regularities and interrelationships that could justify them in developing general theories about economic events and behaviour. They thus contributed more directly to the emergence of a distinctive analytical tradition, a new discipline, than did the multitude of polemicists and persuaders who were adding to the stream of economic pamphlets in the first half of the eighteenth century.

The concept of the economy as a system separate from the political system, for example, and hence the development of a discipline of political economy, took shape quite gradually in eighteenth-century discourse. There were three aspects of economic theorizing that had to come into focus before it could generate a new scientific research programme. The first was the dynamic aspect, the idea that one thing leads to another and that regularly observed associations between economic variables or events carry causal implications capable of justifying predictions. Second, there was the interdependence aspect, the idea that everything depends on everything else in an economic system and that tracing the effects of a particular economic event or policy required assessment of the nature and degrees of dependence between related variables. Third, there was the idea of structural change, that the effects of social and political or economic change on market behaviour depend not only on directions of causation and structures of dependence, but also on the ways incomes and expenditures are redistributed between economic agents, social groups, industrial sectors, or nations.

The dynamic aspect came increasingly into economic analysis early in the eighteenth century: it showed up for example in Law's arguments. The interdependence and structural change aspects were more complex and more difficult to handle with the simple demand and supply techniques of explanation or justification which were by then familiar tools used in systematic discussions of economic policy. They called for more powerful analytical techniques and challenged the theorists to develop higher levels of abstraction. This was the challenge to which Cantillon responded in his *Essai sur la nature du commerce en générale*, in which he attempted a general analysis both of the complex interdependence of the markets for goods and the markets for money, and of the income and price effects associated with different patterns of structural change. In analysing the consequences of an increase in the supply of money he started (as did most of his immediate predecessors and contemporaries) from a definition of money as metallic money, and from the observation that a larger supply of gold or silver was generally associated with a higher level of trade and employment. He traced a causal connection between increased money supply and higher employment, via its effects on demand and profits, and he went on to argue that, by raising domestic prices relative to import prices, an increase in the money supply would generate an excess of imports over exports, draw gold and silver out of the country to finance the unfavourable balance of trade, and thus stimulate forces which would reverse the initial upswing in national economic activity. In short, by theorizing that a money-induced expansion of demand and output was a self-reversing process and by suggesting a systematic explanation for cyclical fluctuations in economic activity and prices, he sowed the seeds for a vision of the economy as a cyclical, self-regulating system.

Cantillon's grasp of the structural dimensions of economic change enabled him to develop an unusually sophisticated analysis of the effects of an increase in the money supply on the rate of interest. For he showed that these effects would vary with the *source* of the increase. For example: 'If the abundance of money in the State comes from the hands of money-lenders it will doubtless bring down the current rate of interest by increasing the number of money-lenders; but if it comes from the intervention of spenders it will have just the opposite effect and will raise the rate of interest by increasing the number of Undertakers who will have employment from this increased business and will need to borrow to equip their business in all classes of interest.' And again: 'When the Prince of the State incurs heavy expenses, such as making war, the rate of interest is raised for two reasons: the first is that this multiplies the number of Undertakers by several new large enterprises for war supplies, and so increasing borrowing. The second is because of the greater risk which war always involves.' And finally: 'When the plentifulness of money in the State is due to a continuous Balance of Trade, this money first passes through the hands of Undertakers, and although it increases consumption it does not fail to bring down the rate of interest, because most of the Undertakers then acquire enough capital to carry on their business without money, and even become lenders of the sums they have gained beyond what they need to carry on their trade.'[2]

What effectively differentiated Cantillon's *Essay* from earlier attempts to answer similar questions was his methodological stance. His discussion of what determined the rate of interest, for example, and his conclusion that it was futile for government to try to regulate the rate by legislative intervenion, was based on a systematic explication of the 'nature of interest'. By focusing his *Essay* on 'the nature of trade in general', he was trying to lay the foundations for a general theory of the market process and to derive from it natural laws governing economic behaviour and economic values. He began with a generalized historical account of the evolution of the socio-economic class structure, identified economic classes whose distinctive behaviour patterns gave them a special role in the circular flow of products and expenditures (e.g. landowners, farmers, merchants and artisans, or under-takers—i.e. entrepreneurs—and hired people), and went on to develop a theory of what later economists were to call 'natural' (as distinct from market) value, a theory hinging on the proposition that 'The price and intrinsic value of a thing in general is the measure of the land and labour which enter into its production.'

This proposition was already a familiar feature of the economic writings (published or privately circulated) available to students of the market economy in the first half of the eighteenth century. A succession of writers shamelessly plagiarized this literature—extracts from Cantillon's manuscript *Essay*, for example, were embodied (often inaccurately) in various published tracts long before the author's version appeared in print in 1755. Those theorists who committed themselves to a search for general principles of economic analysis deliberately built on the researches of their predecessors and advanced their subject by using them critically and selectively. Cantillon, for example, was consciously following in the footsteps of the political arithmeticians, especially Petty.

The original version of his *Essay* contained a statistical supple-ment (now lost) which illustrated or supported his text with quantitative arguments. Significantly, however, Cantillon used Petty's assertion that it was possible to identify a regular proportion (or par) between the relative values of land and labour as the launch pad for a new theory of value, a theory which said 'that the value of the day's work has a relation to the produce of the soil, and that the intrinsic value of any thing may be measured by the quantity of Land used in its production and the quantity of Labour which enters into it, in other words by the quantity of Land of which the produce is allotted to those who worked upon it; and as all the Land belongs to the Prince and the Landowners, all things which have this intrinsic value have it only at their expense.' As the following passage testifies, Cantillon recognized the methodological novelty of his own contribution to the research programme set on foot by the political arithmeticians: 'Sir Wm Petty . . . considers this Par, or Equation between Land and Labour, as the most important consideration in Political Arithmetic, but the research which he has made into it in passing is fanciful and remote from natural laws, *because he has attached himself not to causes and principles, but only to effects as Mr Locke, Mr Davenant and all other English authors who have written on this subject have done after him*' (italics supplied).[3]

There is little doubt that Cantillon's *Essay* was widely read, in French translation as well as in the English original. He was one of the few economic writers whom Adam Smith acknowledged by name and there are too many parallels between the *Essay* and Sir James Steuart's *Principles of Political Œconomy* (first published in 1761) not to suppose that the latter was heavily indebted to it, even if only at second or third hand. But Cantillon's most obvious and direct intellectual legacy went to the French Physiocrats, whose systematic analysis of the economic process provided the rationale for the first school of economic thought. Cantillon's frequent references to the circulation of money and goods, for example, developed in the hands of François Quesnay, the physician, into a direct analogy with the circulation of blood in the human body; and the former's analysis of the interdependence of incomes, expenditures and outputs of pivotal economic classes needed merely an imaginative leap to suggest the latter's famous *Tableau Economique*. There was an obvious link also between physiocratic doctrine and Cantillon's emphasis on the importance of the net agricultural surplus in determining the overall level of economic activity, or of land as the key to intrinsic values of commodities. For these were the assumptions that lay at the heart of the model described by the *Tableau Economique* and gave a rationale for the Physiocrats' characteristic policy prescriptions. As so often in the development of economic thought, however, the simplifications involved in constructing the new model involved a certain distortion of some of the new ideas which originally inspired it. Thus, for example, the Physiocrats treated landowners' rents as the mainspring of economic progress, whereas Cantillon had assigned a substantive role to the profits of the farmers whom he identified as the risk-taking entrepreneurs in the agricultural sector.

By the middle of the eighteenth century, then, the study of political economy had begun to develop a self-consciously objective literature, the authors of which saw themselves as committed to the search for consensual truth—in effect, to a scientific research programme. Sir James Steuart's Inquiry into the *Principles of Political Œconomy*, for example, was subtitled an 'Essay on the science of Domestic Policy in Free Nations' and deliberately abstracted from issues of individual morality in announcing that self-interest was the ruling principle of his subject: 'This is the mainspring and the only motive which a statesman should make use of, to engage a free people to concur in the plans which he lays down for their government.'[4] The idea that moral issues were outside the scope of the economic theorist was becoming generally accepted. 'It may perhaps be urged', Cantillon had written, 'that Undertakers seek to snatch all they can in their calling and get the better of their customers, but this is outside my subject.' Steuart, however, went further in arguing that the principle of self-interest, defined as an underlying regularity in individual economic behaviour, was what made economic management in the public interest feasible: 'Were public spirit, instead of private utility to become the spring of action in the individuals of a well-governed state, I apprehend, it would spoil all . . . the laws of nature would no longer be laws: and were everyone to act for the public, and neglect himself, the statesman would be bewildered.'[5]

The approach to political economy reflected by this passage (and of course by Steuart's subtitle) had recognizable antecedents in earlier writers, such as Petty and Locke, but by the middle decades of the eighteenth century it indicated a divergence from the current trend in economic theorizing and political ideology.

The nub of Steuart's distinctive approach lay in his view of the indispensable role of the state in a changing market economy. For him, the polity and the economy were an indivisible whole, the good statesman was the guardian of the public interest in economic society, and the idea that domestic or foreign markets displayed a natural tendency to equilibrium was pure fantasy. 'In treating every question of political economy,' he wrote, 'I constantly suppose a statesman or the head of the government systematically conducting every part of it, so as to prevent the vicissitudes of manners and innovations, by their natural and immediate effects or consequences from hurting any interest within the commonwealth.' Since 'in a trading and industrious nation time necessarily destroys the perfect balance between work and demand', it was the statesman's duty *at all times to maintain a just proportion between the produce of industry and the quantity of circulating equivalent, in the hands of his subjects, for the purchase of it; that by a steady and judicious administration, he may have it in his power at all times, either to check prodigality and hurtful luxury, or to extend industry and domestic consumption according as the circumstances of the people shall require the one or the other corrective, to be applied to the natural bent and the spirit of the times*.[6]

In short, he envisaged a caring central authority committed to planned, continuous intervention in the free market economy in accordance with generally accepted rules and objectives reflecting the public interest. The rules involved recognition of the natural right of individual economic agents to pursue their own private self-interest at all times, subject only to the needs of the public interest. The public economic objectives included full employment, steady economic growth, and a socially acceptable distribution of incomes. 'A government', he wrote, 'must be continually in action.'

As it happened, however, Steuart had paid for his active part in the Jacobite rebellion of 1745 by a long spell of exile on the Continent. Although he was able to return to Scotland in 1764 he was forced to maintain a low profile in the intellectual community until he was formally pardoned in 1771. As a result, his two-volume *Principles*, the first explicit attempt at a full and objective exposition of the infant science of political economy, was written when he was out of touch with current trends in English political opinion on questions of economic policy and also with the ideological currents that were influencing English or Scottish economic theorists. The earliest reviews showed the way the tide of opinion was moving. The commentator in the 1767 *Critical Review*, for example, wrote: 'We have no idea of a statesman having any connection with the affair and we believe that the superiority which England has at present all over the world, in point of commerce, is owing to her excluding statesmen from the executive part of all commercial concerns.' The spirit of the age was set on course to embrace Adam Smith's view of the economy as a naturally harmonious, self-regulating system in which direct government intervention was more likely to reduce the national level of economic activity than to raise it.

4

The system-builders

A system is an imaginary machine invented to connect together in the fancy those different movements and effects which are in reality performed.

Adam Smith

The moral philosophers who set out to discover the laws under-lying the social order in the early eighteenth century were inspired by the successes of the scientific revolution to adopt similar methods of enquiry to those advocated by the leading natural philosophers. Francis Hutcheson, for example, Adam Smith's predecessor in the chair of moral philosophy at Glasgow, tried to base a new science of ethics on observed regularities in human nature; and his *Inquiry into the Origins of our Ideas of Beauty and Virtue* (1725) hypothesized that human beings tend to put the highest value on those deeds which bring the greatest happiness to the greatest number. David Hume, another leading member of the Scottish Enlightenment, subtitled his *Treatise of Human Nature* (1739) 'an attempt to introduce the experimental method of reasoning into moral subjects'; and he accepted introspection and general human experience as a sufficient source of mental experiments from which to deduce the laws of human behaviour, comparable in their simplicity and stability to Newton's laws of motion.

In France, too, the *philosophes* consciously followed in the footsteps of seventeenth-century natural philosophers, though there, in contrast to Britain, the Cartesian tradition predominated over the Newtonian—at least until Voltaire popularized the empirical philosophy of Newton and Locke. It was the French Physiocrats indeed who were the first true economists. Not only did they call themselves *économistes*, they were the first students of economic behaviour to visualize the economy as an integrated process of causally related, *measurable* market transactions, explicable in terms of a logical, coherent general theory. Like Petty and Locke, for example, François Quesnay (1694–1774) was a practising physician—the personal doctor to Mme la Pompadour and her royal lover Louis XV. He counted himself as a disciple of Descartes, applying rational scientific principles in elaborating a social science which was 'as constant in its principles and as susceptible of demonstration as the most certain physical sciences'. Accordingly, Quesnay set out to map the system of natural laws which he presumed must govern the natural economic order.

Today's economists draw a sharp distinction between two kinds of economic law—the normative 'rules of the game', which define the way individuals and governments *ought* to behave, and the positive regularities in economic behaviour and interrelationships which would enable careful observers to predict the way outputs and prices, or incomes and expenditures, might be expected to respond to the changing patterns of events, institutions, and policy decisions. The Physiocrats' use of the term *droit naturel* embraced both these meanings and sometimes indeed reflected a third concept: the rules which faithful followers of Descartes believed to be naturally imprinted by divine providence in the minds of rational actors in the market economy. Quesnay's essay on *Le droit naturel*, for example, distinguished two kinds of natural law—physical and moral—but like Locke, he seemed to regard them as complementary regularities of nature, implementing the same divine plan: 'All men, all human authorities should be obedient to these sovereign laws established by the supreme being: they are immutable and indisputable and the best laws possible . . .'[1] In general, they seem to have envisaged the 'natural order' of economic affairs not so much as a predetermined actual situation, but as optimal, so that articulating its rules should provide useful criteria to guide the policy choices of individuals and governments in directions which might maximize individual and national prosperity and public revenue.

Most schools of economic thought have started from at least one initial assumption which seems to them so self-evident that it does not require justification. The Physiocrats were no exception.

Their initial hypothesis—which it is not difficult to interpret as a convenient simplification of Cantillon's theory of value (cited above, p. 46)—was that the nation's wealth stemmed ultimately from its natural resources, i.e. land, and hence that land was the exclusive source of the economic surplus on which depended both the taxable capacity of the kingdom and the overall income of its people. They further simplified Cantillon's structural analysis by identifying three pivotal classes in economic society: (1) the farmers who extracted the produce of the soil; (2) the landlords who disposed of nature's bounty, the economic surplus, and thus fed the circular flow of incomes which kept the economic system operating; and (3) the rest of the agents in the market-place (including manufacturers and merchants along with all other income receipients) who played—by virtue of the starting assumption—a non-productive, 'sterile' role in the economic process.

By bringing the system of production (not merely the system of market exchange) into the forefront of their analyses the Physiocrats opened up new perspectives on the processes of economic growth and income distribution. Quesnay, for example, saw more clearly than most of his predecessors the significance of capital investment in raising the productivity of agriculture. He attributed the remarkable upsurge in English incomes over the previous century to the rising productivity of a capital-intensive agricultural industry managed by rational, individualistic farmers. Applying Cantillon's theory of prices he argued that when the products of agriculture were sold in a free market, the prices of food and raw materials would be reduced by competition towards their costs of production, and that the benefits of these low prices would accrue to the whole community, productive and non-productive agents alike.

The principal policy conclusion that the Physiocrats drew from their distinctive model of the economic system was that since national prosperity (and with it the government's revenues) depended on the size of the economic surplus, it was important to free the productive sectors of the economy (by assumption again, the producers of primary products) from all constraints on their marketing operations and all discouragements to investments designed to raise agricultural productivity. They advocated lowering the barriers to international trade, for example, in order to extend the market for French primary products; and they justified measures to redistribute incomes towards the poor and the homeless on the ground that their expenditures would lift the level of effective demand for the output of French farmers.

The Physiocrats produced no comprehensive treatise in defence of their economic doctrine. Their leading exponent, Quesnay, published his economic analysis largely through the medium of short articles written either for the *Encyclopédie* or for the journals contribution to the current debates on economic policy. Nevertheless, they impressed their contemporaries and succeeding generations of political economists with a striking representation of their model of the economic system in the form of a *Tableau Economique*. Various versions of the *Tableau Economique* were produced by Quesnay and his collaborator Mirabeau, but in essence each of them was a mathematically precise way of illustrating and explaining the circular flow of incomes and expenditures linking the three basic classes of economic society—landlords, agriculturalists, and 'unproductive', or 'sterile', agents (including manufacturers and merchants). According to Quesnay, writing to Mirabeau about the first version of the *Tableau* (published in 1758), it was drawn up as a way of 'displaying expenditure and products in a way which is easy to grasp and . . . forming a clear opinion about the organization and disorganization which the government can bring about'. In short, the *Tableau Economique* was designed as an analytical tool which, by imputing precise (not necessarily realistic) numerical values to the incomes and expenditures flowing between the pivotal economic classes, made it possible to visualize the 'whole machinery of circulation' and to trace the consequences of adverse shifts in the distribution of incomes between productive and unproductive classes of society. To quote Mirabeau: 'it is easy to estimate the changes which would take place in the annual reproduction, according as reproductive expenditure or sterile expenditure preponderated. It is easy to estimate them, I say, from the changes which would occur in the *Tableau*.' And he went on to describe a situation in which public policy had the effect of diverting resources out of the productive agricultural sector as equivalent to a situation in which 'the *Tableau* has lost its equilibrium', thereby reducing agricultural productivity and with it the expected economic surplus.

It is possible to exaggerate the logical consistency and analytical sophistication of the model-building technique displayed in the physiocratic *Tableau Economique*. Some twentieth-century writers, for example, struck by the format of the *Tableau*'s matrix of receipts and payments, have likened it to a modern input–output table, which is actually an econometric tool of a very different kind. In the context of the mid eighteenth century, however, Quesnay's imaginative depiction of an economic process operating within a clear quantifiable framework helped to lend scientific status and intellectual appeal to the physiocratic doctrine. In effect what the *Tableau* did was to describe graphically an abstract concept that was already making its appearance in contemporary economic discourse—the idea of visualizing the market economy as a co-ordinated system of interconnected, measurable transactions. It illustrated the way the exchange values arising in a given period of production were spent and received by each of the main classes of society. To scientists and philosophers educated in the Cartesian tradition, the mathematical methodology implicit in the *Tableau Economique* gave credence to the Physiocrats' claim to have discovered the route to eternally valid economic knowledge.

As it turned out, however, the physiocratic school held sway for less than a generation, even in France. There was a drift away from Cartesian rationalism under the influence of Enlightenment philosophers such as Voltaire; and the French Revolution brought to the top an intellectual community which was less likely than its aristocratic predecessors to defer to the authority of dead scholars. In England a doctrine which claimed to be an absolutely certain font of knowledge, but which hinged on the highly restrictive assumption that agriculture was the only really productive sector in the economic system, had little chance of attracting disciples. Nevertheless, the Physiocrats had shown that it was possible to conceptualize an economic system and to describe it in terms of a precise analytical framework within which economic policy prescriptions could be explained and justified. Their achievement inspired Adam Smith to construct a different model of the economic system, based on assumptions which were to seem more realistic in the industrializing, commercialized economies of the late eighteenth or early nineteenth centuries and which generated policy prescriptions that were more acceptable to the liberal politicians of that era.

Adam Smith (1723–90) was primarily an academic and a scholar rather than a business man or a political activist. After entering the University of Glasgow at 14, and graduating at 17, he was awarded a fellowship which would have allowed him to spend at least ten years at Balliol College, Oxford. Actually six years was enough to give him all he wanted from Oxford and he returned to Scotland in 1746. There he moved into a lively and serious intellectual community which was more congenial to an ambitious young scholar than either of the two ancient English universities, whose teachers he was to dismiss as corrupt and lazy because their salaries were drawn from college endowments and altogether independent of their efforts in either teaching or research. In the Scottish universities, by contrast, it was the practice for students to pay their fees directly to the lecturer whose course they chose to attend—which enabled the most effective teacher or reputable scholar to command a premium over lesser academics and offered a financial incentive to intellectual effort.

Smith was invited to lecture at the University of Edinburgh in the academic year 1748/9 on rhetoric and belles-lettres, in a course open to all who were willing to pay the requisite fee, as well as to the mass of matriculated students. His lectures were well received and proved a sufficient success to establish an academic reputation for him. No doubt this was largely responsible for his appointment at the University of Glasgow as Professor of Logic in 1751 and of Moral Philosophy in 1752. There he lectured on theology, ethics, and jurisprudence (a course in which both he and his 'never-to-be-forgotten' teacher Francis Hutcheson dealt with questions of political economy) until late 1763 when he accepted the more lucrative post of tutor to the young Duke of Buccleuch. The new appointment took him to France for four years, thus bringing him into personal contact with the leading members of the physiocratic school, and gave him the stimulus, leisure, and financial security to pursue his own economic researches, culminating in the publication of his *Inquiry into the Nature and the Causes of the Wealth of Nations* (1776). He had already published a major treatise on ethics, *The Theory of Moral Sentiments* (1759), but it was *The Wealth of Nations* which established his reputation for most of his contemporaries and for posterity. When Adam Smith put in the press the first edition of his *Wealth of Nations* he was a mature scholar in his early fifties who had been reading, writing, and arguing with the leading philosophers of his day for more than a quarter of a century, focusing on various aspects of what contemporary thinkers called the 'science of man'. His lectures on economic questions and his broad-ranging inquiry into the nature and causes of national wealth were only part of a much wider research programme which he did not find time to complete. It may be significant that although both his *Theory of Moral Sentiments* and his *Wealth of Nations* went into several editions before he died, he spent less time and effort in rethinking and revising the latter than he did the former. The last major revision in *The Wealth of Nations* was for the third edition, which appeared in 1784, but Smith was still seriously revising his *Theory of Moral Sentiments* in 1790, the year he died.

But if Adam Smith did not regard his comprehensive treatise on the conditions of economic progress as the most important of his contributions to the science of man, his most influential disciples and successive generations of economists certainly did. Most historians of economic thought have agreed in attributing fundamental importance to it as laying the foundation for the discipline of political economy. Some twentieth-century writers indeed have argued that Smith's distinctive vision of the economic system established a paradigm for modern economic analysis which has survived in all its essentials up to the present day. There is no doubt that the *Wealth of Nations*, the first edition of which was sold out in six months, made a powerful immediate impression on the educated élite of Europe and North America in the late eighteenth and early nineteenth centuries. It launched an economic research programme which is still in progress, and it justified a package of policy prescriptions which are being justified on essentially similar lines more than two centuries later.

Smith himself made it clear that he was engaged in an ongoing research programme within an established branch of knowledge whose validity depended on its effectiveness in providing usable advice to policy makers, and that he intended radically to reconstruct the analytical framework on which leading writers on economic affairs traditionally erected their arguments. Book IV of *The Wealth of Nations*, for example, is entitled 'Of systems of political œconomy' and begins with a succinct, two-paragraph introduction defining the objectives of the discipline and identifying the two contemporary systems of ideas which he proposed to update:

Political œconomy, considered as a branch of a statesman or legislator, proposes two distinct objects; first, to provide a plentiful revenue or subsistence for the people, or more properly to enable them to provide such a revenue or subsistence for themselves; and secondly to supply the state or commonwealth with a revenue sufficient for the public services. It proposes to enrich both the people and the sovereign.

The different progress of opulence in different ages and nations has given occasion to two different systems of political œconomy with regard to enriching the people. The one may be called the system of commerce, the other that of agriculture. I shall endeavour to explain both as fully and distinctly as I can, and I shall begin with the system of commerce. It is the modern system and is best understood in our own country and in our own times.[2]

The 'system of commerce', more often referred to subsequently as the 'mercantile system', is what was later dubbed mercantilism and Smith devoted more than a quarter of the two substantial volumes of *The Wealth of Nations* to a critique of the arguments which he subsumed under that heading. The 'system of agriculture', which he attributed to the Physiocrats, was dealt with relatively briefly in a single chapter, on the grounds that it had had little influence on contemporary economic thinking outside France: 'That system which represents the produce of land as the sole source of the revenue and wealth of every country has, so far as I know, never been adopted by any nation, and it at present exists only in the speculations of a few men of great learning and ingenuity in France.'[3]

In both cases, however, the main burden of his critique was the same. It was that all attempts to promote national economic progress by restricting the activities of individuals operating in fully competitive markets were destined to be self-defeating, so that

every system which endeavours, either, by extraordinary encouragements, to draw towards a particular species of industry a greater share of the capital of society than what would naturally go to it; or by extraordinary restraint to force from a particular species of industry some share of capital which would otherwise be employed in it, is in reality subversive of the great purpose which it means to promote. It retards instead of accelerating, the progress of the society towards real wealth and greatness; and diminishes, instead of increasing the real value of the annual produce of its land and labour.[4]

In short, the message was that there was an underlying order in the capitalist market economy which had a natural tendency to enrich the people. Governments concerned to promote national wealth should work within that order rather than against it, so allowing it to exert its full beneficial force.

The fact that Adam Smith's dramatic vision of a self-regulating economic system had superficial attractions to the many eighteenth-century producers and traders who chafed against a multitude of government restrictions on their economic activities does not explain its success in winning over the broader intellectual community. It was not distinguished by striking novelties in its theoretical or conceptual techniques of analysis, or by novel philosophical insights, or by unexpected empirical observations. On the contrary, it is arguable that *The Wealth of Nations* became an instant bestseller largely because it was so sharply tuned in to the spirit of the age. When David Hume, on reading the first edition, doubted whether it would enjoy the kind of popular success recently afforded to, say, Gibbon's *Decline and Fall of the Roman Empire*, he misjudged the extent to which the Scottish professor was reflecting current trends in educated opinion. A text which stood so patently on the shoulders of the intellectual giants on which the existing stock of economic wisdom was generally believed to depend had built into it a certain generalized plausibility. Serious academics, moreover, were impressed by Smith's determination to apply an apparently scientific methodology to the science of man and by his ability to account for the behaviour of individuals in the market place, or the comparative growth experience of nations, on the basis of a few general laws or axioms, just as Newton had done in explaining the movements of the planets. According to Smith's pupil and leading academic disciple, Dugald Stewart, for example: '. . . the merit of such a work as Mr Smith's is to be estimated less from the novelty of the principles it contains, than from the manner in which they are unfolded in their proper order and connexion.'

For most well-informed observers, Adam Smith's arguments gained credibility as a result of his tendency to prefer simple theories to complex ones, to analyse human behaviour in terms that would seem wholly familiar to the decision-taking agents themselves, and to illustrate his theories by reference to well-documented historical or comparative data and readily observed contemporary events or circumstances. For politicians in particular, and indeed for all those with an active interest in questions of national economic policy-making, what gave *The Wealth of Nations* its special claim to attention was the fact that it was a tract for the times. It focused on the economic policy issues currently accepted as being of primary importance. It was alive to the conflicts of interest in economic society as well as optimistic about the potential of a commercial economy for achieving improvements in the quality and material content of human standards of living. And while it presumed certain identifiable constancies and regularities in human motives and behaviour patterns, it recognized that the march of events and the character of economic institutions would produce intertemporal and international variations in the ways individuals typically responded to the economic opportunities confronting them and in the extent to which governments could usefully promote national economic development.

But for the politicians the most attractive feature of Adam Smith's *Wealth of Nations* was that it gave scientific credentials to a policy stance which was in tune with the ideology glamourized by the enlightenment philosophers—the ideology of economic liberalism. The story has often been told of a reception held in 1787 at the London house of Henry Dundas, to which Adam Smith, then on his last visit to the capital, arrived late. The distinguished company, including such notables as the younger Pitt (then Prime Minister), Henry Addington (Speaker of the House of Commons), William Wilberforce, and George Grenville, rose spontaneously to greet the Scottish professor and remained standing. 'Be seated, gentlemen,' said Smith. 'No,' replied Pitt, 'We will stand till you are first seated for we are all your scholars.'

How far Smith actually did apply a Newtonian scientific method to his inquiry into the nature and causes of the wealth of nations is debatable. He did not discuss his own methodology, perhaps because he had already made his views clear elsewhere, particularly in the long (posthumously published) essay on *The History of Astronomy*, as well as in his well-known *Theory of Moral Sentiments*. From these writings we can infer that he accepted a Newtonian world-view and that he intended to apply a Newtonian scientific method in studying the economic system. The essence of the Newtonian world-view was that it started from two axioms, two articles of faith about the real world in its social as well as its physical aspects: (1) that it was characterized by uniformities and constancies which were sufficiently regular to have the force of laws of nature; and (2) that it was designed and guided by an intelligent creator. Taken together, these initial premises implied that there was a systematic, god-given harmony in the operations of the universe and that the task of the social scientist investigating a discrete section or sub-system of it was to identify the fundamentally simple axioms and laws on which it hinged, to classify the strategic variables which set it in motion and to analyse the structural relationships of cause and effect which gave that particular system its coherence and predictability. For the social scientist it involved establishing those constant principles of human nature which were sufficiently powerful in their effects on individual behaviour to provide an effective starting point for a deductive chain of reasoning.

That the investigative methods of the social scientist differed in significant respects from those of the natural scientists was obvious enough to eighteenth-century thinkers concerned with the science of man. For one thing, their empirical enquiries took a different form. Evidently, for example, the observations which would allow the crucial fundamental principles of human nature to be established had to be based primarily on introspection; but to philosophers convinced of the existence of a divine plan and a law-governed universe, this in no way invalidated the objectivity of the moral or social sciences. On the contrary, it was commonly believed that human beings were more likely to reach a consensus on these subjective data drawn from personal experience than on observations of inanimate nature or non-human animals. Endowed with this privileged access to the secrets of human nature, the student of society could, however, borrow the mechanical analogies developed by physical scientists to find purposeful coherence in the jigsaw of behaviour patterns and events. As Adam Smith put it in his *Theory of Moral Sentiments*: 'Human society when we contemplate it in a certain abstract and philosophical light appears like a great, an immense machine, whose regular and harmonious movements produce a thousand agreeable effects.' Moreover, the social scientist had a further advantage over his natural science counterpart in that he did not require either a telescope or a laboratory to provide the empirical data necessary for the derivation or confirmation of his theories of cause and effect. The facts of personal experience and the historical record were at every scholar's disposal.

The fundamental principle of human nature on which Smith based his model of the economic system was the principle of self-interest. Politicians and academics alike could readily swallow the proposition that the prime objective motivating the typical individual in a modern commercialized economy was to maximize his own gains from trade. Combined, however, with belief in a divine plan for society as a whole and with the theory that the rational pursuit of personal gain in a freely competitive market tends to maximize national wealth, it generated a novel but seductive system of ideas in support of economic liberalism. According to Smith, for example: 'The natural effort of every individual to better his own condition, when suffered to exert itself with freedom and security, is so powerful a principle that it is alone, and without any assistance, not only capable of carrying on the society to wealth and prosperity, but of surmounting a hundred impertinent obstructions with which the folly of human laws too often incumbers its operations.'[5]

In a world where governments intervened constantly and often either arbitrarily or corruptly in the processes of production, consumption, and trade, the doctrine that such interference was not merely unnecessary to promote economic growth, but was often actually inimical to it, had obvious attractions for an educated community which put a high value on economic freedom. Smith insisted, for example, that the capitalist entrepreneur who was 'naturally' motivated to maximize his profits had a permanent incentive to increase output, reduce his operational risks, invest in the most lucrative areas of production or trade (generally in domestic rather than foreign industry), and concentrate his productive efforts on supplying the goods in greatest demand. In effect: 'Every individual is continually exerting himself to find out the most advantageous employment for whatever capital he can command. It is his own advantage indeed and not that of the society, which he has in view. But the study of his own advantage naturally, or rather necessarily leads him to prefer that employment which is most advantageous to the society.'[6] And after giving realistic illustrations of such behaviour, Smith concluded with the following passage which became the ideological manifesto for classical political economy:

As every individual, therefore, endeavours as much as he can to employ his capital in the support of domestick industry, and so to direct that industry that its produce may be of the greatest value; every individual necessarily labours to render the annual revenue of the society as great as he can. He generally, indeed, neither intends to promote the publick interest nor knows how much he is promoting it. By preferring the support of domestick to that of foreign industry, he intends only his own security; and by directing that industry in such a manner as its produce may be of the greatest value, he intends only his own gain, and he is in this, as in many other cases, led by an invisible hand to promote an end which was no part of his intention.[7]

The vision of a collectivity of acquisitive individuals combining into a just and stable society had appeared often enough in the philosophical debates of the late seventeenth and early eighteenth centuries. It took its most cynical form in Mandeville's *Fable of the Bees*, which argued that 'Private Vices by the dextrous Management of a Skilful Politician may be turned into Public Benefits.' As rationalized by Adam Smith, however, it became more than a satirical metaphor. It dramatized the paradigm for a new discipline. Starting from a readily intelligible problem situation, focused on how to promote national economic development, it defined the main object of the policies which improvements in economic knowledge were designed to serve, as that of 'enriching the people', more specifically, raising the level of national income per head of the population. It defined the central focus of economic analysis; for Smith and his immediate successors, the classical political economists, analysing the process of production took priority over the process of exchange. It classified the strategic economic variables into factors of production—land, labour, and capital—whose individual components were recognizable actors in the capitalist market economy (those who lived by rent, those who lived by wages, and those who lived by profits) and whose products or incomes summed exhaustively to the value of total national product at the macro-economic level. It added to the existing corpus of economic knowledge a substantial if somewhat eclectic theoretical element, which offered an integrated explanation for the most fundamental of economic problems—the problem of devising a theory of value to account for both the intrinsic and the market values of commodities—together with an essentially new theory of economic growth.

The central importance of the theory of value for political economists arises from its ethical implications. Modern economists who attach importance to developing a 'value-free' science of economics have tended to obscure this connection. But Adam Smith, for whom political economy was a branch or application of ethics, found it necessary to construct a theory which explained not merely the mechanism by which commodities acquired their market prices, but also the teleological justice of the results. He faced the problem squarely in Book I of *The Wealth of Nations* by posing three questions:

In order to investigate the principles which regulate the exchangeable value of commodities, I shall endeavour to shew, First, what is the real measure of this exchangeable value; or wherein consists the real price of commodities, Secondly what are the different parts of which this real price is composed or made up, And lastly, what are the different circumstances which sometimes raise some or all of these different parts of the price above, and sometime sink them below their natural or ordinary rate; or what are the causes which sometimes hinder the market price, that is, the actual price of commodities from coinciding exactly with what may be called their natural price.[8]

His answer to the first of these questions was that the 'real' price was the price a commodity would fetch *naturally*, when the market was in long-term competitive equilibrium, so that producers were supplying exactly as much of the commodity in question as consumers were willing to buy. He defined the equilibrium situation in Newtonian terms: 'The natural price, therefore, is, as it were, the central price, to which the prices of all commodities are continually gravitating. Different accidents may sometimes keep them suspended a good deal above it, and sometimes force them down even somewhat below it. But whatever may be the obstacles which hinder them from settling in this center of repose and continuance, they are constantly tending towards it.'

The second question he dealt with by postulating a cost of production theory of value, defining the natural price of a commodity as being 'neither more nor less than what is sufficient to pay the rent of the land, the wages of the labour, and the profits of the stock employed in raising, preparing and bringing it to market, according to their natural rates'.

The third question, which distinguished the actual or market price of a commodity from its real or natural price (i.e. value), he answered by listing the reasons why there might be disequilibrium in the demand and supply for a particular commodity—for example, persistent imperfections in the market (due say to monopolies or government intervention) or transitory shifts due to accidental changes in the conditions of supply or of 'effectual' demand. He argued, for example, that 'where there was perfect liberty' the principle of self-interest would impel producers to supply as much as the market would take, but that 'sometimes particular accidents, sometimes natural causes and sometimes particular regulations of police, may, in many commodities, keep the market price, for a long time together, a good deal above the natural price'. On the other hand, if demand fell, forcing market price below the cost of production for a particular commodity, there would be a tendency for those who were losing by this shortfall in their returns to move their land, labour, or capital to more lucrative employments—again, of course, provided that they were left free to do so.

The crucial feature of Adam Smith's theory of value then was that it associated with a freely competitive market the economic benefits of minimizing prices to consumers and maximizing returns to producers. In that system of perfect liberty in which the invisible hand was allowed to produce its full harmonious effects unhindered by government intervention or producer's monopolies, the self-seeking activities of individuals could be shown to promote wealth and prosperity for the nation as a whole. It was a theory of value, moreover, which laid a firm foundation for Smith's distinctive theory of growth and helped to justify a *laissez-faire* policy stance for governments concerned to reconcile the objectives of economic justice and national economic growth. By identifying the annual produce of the nation with the sum of individual revenues (wages, profit, and rents) and treating national output per head as the key growth variable (rather than, say, the agricultural surplus on which the Physiocrats had focused) Smith was able to integrate a theory of value with a theory of growth and to use both in support of his case for economic liberalism.

The ability to synthesize—to construct a coordinated system of economic thought by process of selection among currently familiar concepts, hypotheses, and opinions—was Adam Smith's special talent. He had inherited from his mercantilist mentors, for example, the assumption that the ultimate source of wealth—at both the individual and the national level of analysis—was human labour. But the theory of economic growth which he spun out of this conventional starting point was more fruitful than any of its predecessors—largely no doubt because he kept it firmly rooted in a socio-economic analysis of the process of production rather than of exchange. He gave it a historical dimension by adopting the notion, already familiar in the Enlightenment tradition, that human societies typically progress through a series of stages, each characterized by the way it satisfied its subsistence needs, that is, by its mode of production—hunting, pasturage, farming, and commerce. True, this was what Dugald Stewart was to describe as 'conjectural history; but Smith gave it empirical substance by copious illustrations drawing on intertemporal or international comparisons from the real world. The historical argument served in effect to sharpen his focus on the final stage of economic development, the modern economy whose conditions of economic progress he wanted to explain and prescribe policies for. He identified it by three dynamic characteristics: first, that it produced annually more than was necessary to meet the subsistence needs of the people; second, that a large proportion of its output was produced for sale on national or international markets rather than for consumption by the producer or his dependants; and third, that it showed an inherent tendency to increase its annual economic surplus. It was the last of these characteristics that called for explanation and for which Adam Smith constructed a theory of growth and proposed his policy package.

For the inhabitants of the modern commercialized economy the prospects of continuing improvements in national output per head depended, according to Smith, on the interactions between the division of labour, technical knowledge, capital accumulation, and population increase. Specialization raised labour productivity by increasing worker dexterity, saving time in passing between productive operations, and facilitating the invention of labour-saving devices and machinery. Increased labour productivity led to increasing profits, higher capital accumulation, more employment opportunities, and greater scope for division of labour. The rate of increase of national income determined the extent of the domestic market for manufactured goods and with it the scope for specialization of labour and the level of profits. The rate of increase of population governed the number sharing in the national output and hence the size of the annual economic surplus available for capital accumulation.

The strategic elements in Smith's theory of growth were thus the division of labour and capital accumulation. For as long as product per head grew faster than consumption per head, the annual economic surplus would continue to generate a rising demand for labour and a growing population. Smith accepted the existence of long-term limits to growth set by a country's natural resources; that is, he saw a stop to growth when a country 'had acquired that full complement of riches which the nature of its soil and climate and its situation with respect to other countries allowed it to acquire'. But he was not much concerned by that distant horizon. His more immediate interest lay in identifying the short-term and insurmountable limits set by political factors constraining the inherent tendency of a commercial economy to allocate its scarce productive resources in the most profitable ways open to it.

The *Wealth of Nations* established the status of political economy as a distinct branch of knowledge by giving it, for the first time, its own comprehensive textbook analysing the economy as a coherent system with laws of motion comparable in their regularity and internal consistency to the laws which Newton had discovered for the solar system. It located the discipline with the moral and political sciences as a 'branch of the science of a statesman or legislator'. It identified the central economic problem as being to explain and prescribe policies for the growth of national wealth. It used the existing corpus of economic knowledge in erecting a systematic framework of theory and in relating it to realistic categories, events, behaviour patterns and policy problems. Most important of all, it justified an overall view of the national economy as a self-regulating system and associated it with a doctrine concerning the role of the State in that system—a doctrine that was to have a long-term influence on the development of the new discipline.

In the later debates on the role of the State *The Wealth of Nations* has frequently been cited in support of an extreme *laissez-faire* position, the view that it is the business of government to leave things alone and allow those who wield the effective power in modern capitalism freedom to take their self-interested decisions without hindrance. Nor is it hard to find passages that serve this ideological purpose, for Adam Smith was reacting forcefully against the multitude of arbitrary, often ineffective or counter-productive, generally cost-raising regulations that eighteenth-century monarchies commonly imposed on producers or consumers. He was scathing about the incompetence or corruption of politicians and about their vulnerability to pressure from vested interest. He was equally scathing, as it happened, about the propensity of capitalists to underpay their employees and to use their privileged position in the economy to maximize their incomes in ways that militated against the public interest. But the main scientific objective of his work was to inform and advise those legislators who were serious in their concern for the public interest and impartial as between conflicting economic classes. He did not suppose that his vision of an economic 'system of natural liberty' was an accurate description of the way the modern economy actually operated. On the contrary, it was an abstraction, a goal to be kept in view rather than reached. Its importance as a component of his advice to governments was that it spelt out his assumption that there was a natural order in the social (as in the cosmic) system. The danger, as he saw, was that clever and honest statesmen (for instance, Colbert in France) would attempt to impose their own plans for economic development in such ignorance of the divine plan for the economic system that they would create disorder rather than order. It was a theme he had already developed in his *Theory of Moral Sentiments* when criticizing the 'man of system', with his own ideal plan for government, who

seems to think that he can arrange the different members of a great society with as much ease as the hand arranges the different pieces upon a chessboard. He does not consider that the pieces upon the chessboard have no other principles of motion besides that which the hand imposes upon them; but that in the great chessboard of human society, every single piece had a principle of motion of its own, altogether different from that which the legislature might choose to impress upon it. If those two principles coincide and act in the same direction, the game of human society will go on easily and harmoniously, and it is very likely to be happy and successful. If they are opposite or different, the game will go on miserably and the society must be at all times in the highest degree of disorder.[9]

The abstract quality of Smith's 'system of natural liberty' is clearly expressed in *The Wealth of Nations*. His succinct statement of the role of the State in the economic system, for example, was explicitly predicated on the assumption that all imperfections in the market had been eliminated. Then:

According to the system of natural liberty, the sovereign has only three duties to attend to; three duties of great importance, indeed, but plain and intelligible to common understandings: first, the duty of protecting the society from the violence and invasion of other independent societies; secondly the duty of protecting, as far as possible, every member of the society from the injustice or oppression of every other member of it, or the duty of establishing an exact administration of justice; and, thirdly, the duty of erecting and maintaining certain publick works and certain publick institutions, which it can never be for the interest of any individual, or small number of individuals, to erect and maintain; because the profit could never repay the expense to any individual or small number of individuals, though it may frequently do much more than repay it to a great society.[10]

In effect, these were general guidelines designed to encourage legislators to work towards (rather than against) the growth-promoting tendencies inherent in the divine plan for the economy—not a warning against any kind of government intervention in the processes of production or trade. Indeed the need to raise revenues to finance the performance of the first and second duties of government clearly implied substantial intervention in the market-place, while the third duty—that of filling the investment and institutional gaps left by private enterprise—opened a very wide role (even at the theoretical level of analysis) for government to play in the economic system. At the practical, policy-formulating level, of course, Adam Smith was more a realist than a polemicist—a fact that probably went a long way towards explaining the wide success of *The Wealth of Nations*. Even his powerful arguments for free trade were qualified by the realization that there were economic as well as political or financial limitations to their practical implementation. 'To expect, indeed', he concluded, 'that the freedom of trade should ever be entirely restored in Great Britain is as absurd as to expect that an Oceana or Utopia should ever be established in it. Not only the prejudices of the publick, but what is much more unconquerable, the private interests of many individuals, irresistibly oppose it.'[11]

Nevertheless, the general reputation of *The Wealth of Nations* as a fount of commonsensical wisdom was given an early boost in Britain and on the Continent, not only because it caught the liberal tide flowing from the Enlightenment, but also because its advice to legislators seemed so successful in its practical consequences. The Younger Pitt, who became Prime Minister in 1783, at the teachable age of 25, was deeply impressed by the Scottish professor's doctrine of trade liberalization. He took an early opportunity to reduce the swingeing duties on tea from 119 to 12½ per cent and was rewarded by a substantial increase in dutiable imports as the smugglers lost their incentive to bring in an article of mass consumption; it was also believed at the time that the lucrative illicit trade in tea had brought with it a contraband trade in a number of other commodities which found their way into taxable channels when tea ceased to finance the smugglers. In 1786 the Eden Treaty to relax restraints on trade between Britain and France was signed in the teeth of mercantile opposition on both sides of the Channel and went on to surprise its opponents with the self-evident advantages it had for both countries. The political opposition to Pitt's concurrent attempts to free trade between Britain and Ireland was more successful in frustrating his objective, but he might well have won the day had not the outbreak of the revolutionary and Napoleonic wars abruptly transformed the agenda of policy makers.

5

The dismal scientists

Metaphysics and enquiries into moral and political science, have become little else than vain attempts to revive exploded superstitions, or sophisms like those of Mr Malthus, calculated to lull the oppressors of mankind into a security of everlasting triumph.

Percy Bysshe Shelley

In comprehensiveness, relevance, and sheer breadth and depth of scholarship, Adam Smith's textbook for political economy had no rival among its precursors, nor indeed amongst its followers until J.S. Mill set out to match its scope and update its content with his *Principles of Political Economy with some of their Applications to Social Philosophy* (1848). The intellectual community of economists which took shape in the first half of the nineteenth century, however, and for which *The Wealth of Nations* represented a common core, shared with the statesmen and legislators a significantly different set of problems from those that had confronted Adam Smith in the third quarter of the eighteenth century. Accordingly, its active practitioners found themselves developing a research programme which made so many changes in the original Smithian model that its author might have found it hard to recognize his own contribution to orthodox classical political economic doctrine.

There were three reasons why the problems were transformed for those seeking or offering advice on economic policy in the 1790s and beyond. The first was a demographic revolution which set off a dramatic and sustained upsurge in population growth and which showed up not only in Britain but in underdeveloped Ireland, the newly independent United States, as well as in northwestern Europe generally. The second was the outbreak of the French revolutionary and Napoleonic wars, which lasted until

1815 and had a more disturbing effect on the economy of Britain and its main commercial rivals than any other eighteenth- or nineteenth-century war. The third was an acceleration of the process of industrialization in Britain (and to a lesser extent in Western Europe), a process which was beginning to exhibit a marked impact on the structure and pace of British economic development by the end of the century. These three revolutionary occurrences interacted to produce an unprecedented and unexpected degree of social and economic change, thus posing urgent and often confusing problems for British policy makers.

The social effects of the population explosion were becoming obvious before the first British Census of Population revealed its surprising dimensions in 1801. The evidence of concern lay in a stream of pamphlets and books published in the second half of the eighteenth century to document the increasing pressure of underemployment, low wages, and rising prices on working class standards of living—culminating in Sir Frederic Eden's *The State of the Poor*, published in four large volumes in 1797. In these circumstances the orthodox mercantilist, pro-natalist doctrine became an anachronism.

It was against this background of intensifying population pressure that T. R. Malthus (1766–1834) published his first essay on population in 1798, elaborating a theory of the relationship between population and natural resources. The first version of Malthus's famous *Essay*—as its full title reveals—was not written as a contribution to the perennial population debate, but as an attempt to inject some realism into the moralistic theorizing on human perfectibility associated with the romantic interpretation of the French Revolution. He called it 'An essay on the principle of population as it affects the future improvement of society, with remarks on the speculations of Mr Godwin, M. Condorcet and other writers'. Condorcet had sketched a stage theory of human development in which the ultimate stage, a golden age inaugurated by the French Revolution, would, he argued, eliminate all inequalities of wealth, education, sex, opportunity, and language and thus solve, at a stroke, all the major social problems of the era. Godwin rejected every form of governmental or legal restriction on individual freedom and argued that if all rational human beings were left free to develop naturally there 'will be no war, no crimes, no administration of justice, as it is called, and no government. Besides this there will be neither disease, anguish melancholy nor resentment.' In this Utopian state the dissipation of the sexual urge and the total conquest of death would eventually eliminate the problems of over-population and poverty.

In opposition to these bizarre 'speculations on the perfectibility of man and society' Malthus put forward a 'principle of population' based on the assumption that human beings have a natural propensity to reproduce themselves faster than they can increase the basic means of subsistence. There was nothing new about the basic proposition. It had been epigrammatically expressed by Cantillon: 'Men multiply like Mice in a barn when grain is plentiful.' It had been spelt out more ponderously, with the aid of a mechanical analogy by Sir James Steuart:

Thus the generative faculty resembles a spring with a loaded weight, which always exerts itself in proportion to the diminution of resistance. When food has remained some time without any augmentation or diminution, generation will carry numbers as high as possible: if then food come to be diminished, the spring is overpowered; the force of it becomes less than nothing. Inhabitants will diminish, at least, in proportion to the overcharge. If upon the other hand, food be increased, the spring which stood at 0, will begin to exert itself in proportion as the resistance diminishes, people will begin to be better fed; they will multiply, and in proportion as they increase in numbers the food will become scarce again.[1]

Adam Smith, like most eighteenth-century philosophers, took it for granted as a well-known biological fact and then used it as the starting point for discussing the factors affecting the supply of labour and the level of wages in comparing countries at different levels of development. Malthus made the point in the mathematical terminology which came naturally enough to a Cambridge Wrangler (graduate with first class honours in the Mathematical Tripos) and which commended it to the educated élite: 'Population when unchecked, increases in a geometrical ratio. Subsistence increases only in an arithmetical ratio.'

It is, on the face of it, surprising that this absurdly over-precise statement of an axiom which in its more general form was commonly accepted by eighteenth-century thinkers should have made its author famous. The first edition of the *Essay* was published anonymously and created a sensation. Malthus was glad to put his name to the second, much expanded, version published five years later—significantly after the results of the 1801 Census were known. In 1805 he was appointed the first professor of history and political economy, not at a university but at the newly established College for cadets of the East India Company, and his book (now crammed with historical and international illustrations) became a nineteenth-century classic. Both Charles Darwin and Alfred Russel Wallace claimed to have been inspired to develop the biological theory of evolution (which they arrived at simultaneously and independently) after reading Malthus's *Essay*.

In the original success of the *Essay*, timing was of course crucial. The policy problems created by the distress of the poor were at the forefront of public debate in the 1790s and remained high on the social agenda as wartime inflation, together with the structural shifts produced by war and its aftermath, exacerbated existing problems of low wages and technological unemployment associated with industrialization and economic change. An Act of 1795 which had allowed JPs to prescribe outdoor relief for the able-bodied poor in temporary distress was followed by the spread of local policies (beginning in the Berkshire village of Speenhamland) to supplement low wages and to fix the individual pauper's entitlement by reference to the number of his dependants and the price of bread. The sentiments which encouraged the spread of what has since become known as the Speenhamland system reflected a mixture of general humanitarianism and fear of social disorder (a fear intensified by recent events in France); but enlightened statesmen, such as the Younger Pitt, appealed to justice. 'Let us', he said in a speech to the House of Commons in 1796, 'make relief in cases where there are a number of children a matter of right and honour, instead of a ground of opprobrium and contempt. This will make a large family a blessing, and not a curse; and this will draw a proper line of distinction between those who are able to provide for themselves by their labour, and those who after having enriched their country with a number of children, have a claim on its assistance for support.' This, however, was a line of argument which the new breed of economists were to scorn as being at variance with the laws of political economy.

It has since been shown that the Speenhamland system was less generously and less generally implemented than was intended, but the opposition of property holders to policies that would further add to the rising burden of poor rates was sufficient to frustrate Pitt's humanitarian plans for reform of the Poor Laws. To the running debate on poor relief which persisted through the war and post-war period and culminated in the punishing Poor Law Amendment Act of 1834, Malthus's *Essay* made a significant contribution. Its first edition argued in effect that the miseries produced by excessive procreation—starvation, crime, war, vice—were unavoidable. It was nature (reflected in the principle of population) rather than social injustice, that was responsible for extremes of poverty, and that regulated the population excess in these miserable ways. True, in the later editions of his *Essay* Malthus modified this bleak picture by admitting an alternative check to population growth—'moral restraint'. He did not, of course, go as far as Jeremy Bentham and the philosophical radicals in advocating the legalization and spread of contraception (which for Parson Malthus was vice) so that his policy prescriptions remained unrelentingly hard: 'I feel little doubt in my own mind,' he wrote, 'that if the poor laws had never existed, though there might have been a few more instances of severe distress, yet the aggregate mass of happiness among the common people would have been greater than it is at present.' It was an argument which persuaded William Pitt to abandon his Poor Law Reform Bill and with which Ricardo was unequivocally in favour. The hardliners in the Poor Law debate were thus able to base their opposition to all government policies aimed at alleviating poverty on the objective laws of political economy. To the extent that the economic system was naturally self-regulating, man-made attempts to relieve the corrective pattern of misery could only worsen the condition of the poor. Only the threat of revolution justified the authorities in intervening to palliate a poverty which was a signal to its victims that their own industry, prudence, foresight, and moral restraint could alone effect a permanent improvement in their living standards.

Most nineteenth-century economists—even those who found the more extreme Malthusian versions of the population principle excessively naive—accepted the hardline policy implications that were generally associated with it. Nassau Senior, for example, the first Oxford Professor of Political Economy, was one of the architects of the Poor Law Amendment Act, by which central government sought to force the local authorities to respect the laws of political economy and to administer poor relief in ways that would not encourage the idle and improvident members of the working classes to become dependent on the taxpaying classes whose savings were needed to finance the national growth process. The Act was designed to confine poor relief to maintenance in efficiently draconian workhouse institutions, ruthlessly splitting up families and expressly prohibiting outdoor relief to the able-bodied unemployed, on the ground that the most effective way of raising the standard of living of the working classes was to give them the strongest possible incentive to help themselves. In the event, the actual implementation of the Act by the local authorities was less complete. But the idea that the laws of political economy demanded punishment for poverty, rather than a more just redistribution of incomes from rich to poor, injected an ideological bias into economic debate, which could only be justified by detaching orthodox political economy from ethical considerations and which has never lost its power to persuade some policymakers that governmental efforts to equalize incomes are inevitably counter-productive. To the Romantics and socialist Radicals it provided an important part of the evidence for the view that the 'dismal science' led to intolerably unjust policy prescriptions.

The other set of policy problems which raised the temperature of economic debate during the long wars were questions of monetary policy. Adam Smith had not made a significant contribution to ideas on money, credit, and banking policy. He had inherited from Locke, Cantillon, and Hume a substantial body of theory on the way the money economy worked and it commanded a sufficient consensus in the intellectual community for which he was writing to provide an acceptable basis for his own analyses and prescriptions in this area. His main concern was with the factors determining the growth of *real* national incomes and expenditures (aggregate output and consumption of physical commodities). In this context he found it convenient to treat money as a neutral rather than a dynamic factor in the process of production. 'The sole function of money', he assumed, 'is to circulate consumable goods.' So, by ignoring the function of money as a store of value, and tacitly assuming that the supply of money was determined by the value of goods circulating through the economy, he was able to argue that in a modern, efficient credit system (efficient in the sense that loans were made only against metallic money deposits, mainly by substantial, reputable bankers dealing in large notes and largely to creditworthy borrowers) the dangers, at the national level, of an excessive money supply were in practice negligible. Competition and self-interest would ensure that imprudent lenders and borrowers would be few in number and quick either to accept the discipline or to drop out of the modern money market.

During the 1790s, however, and particularly after the outbreak of war in 1793, it became apparent that maintenance of monetary stability was a problem which central government could not ignore. Evidently, understanding the complex interrelationships between money, interest, exchange rates, and prices called for a more sophisticated theory than was contained in *The Wealth of Nations*. For one thing, the nation's banking system had changed in structure and behaviour on lines that could hardly have been foreseen when Adam Smith was researching his book. For another, the increased government expenditures necessitated by the war outstripped those of any previous conflict, both in absolute scale and relatively to national income as well as to the annual rate of economic growth. For yet another, the normal confidence which sustains the expectations and orders the behaviour of buyers and sellers in either commodity or money markets is vulnerable to the sudden shocks and temporary setbacks associated with a major war. Moreover, since instability in the value of the nation's money supply directly threatens its ability to conduct military operations abroad, or to subsidise allies, questions of national security were involved in the problems of monetary policy.

In the hundred years that followed its establishment in 1694 the Bank of England had become the centre of a loosely co-ordinated national credit structure and the leading monetary authority. It was the sole joint stock bank in England and the only source of bank notes in London. Outside the metropolis, the Banks of Ireland and of Scotland and a large number of country banks of England, Ireland, and Scotland also exercised rights to issue their own banknotes (often secured on deposits of Bank of England notes) without any legal restraint other than the interest maximum of 5 per cent imposed by the Usury Laws. As the government's bank the Bank of England found the finance for major public expenditure by raising fixed-interest loans with interest charges secured on specific taxes; and it paid the government's creditors with bank notes which were effective substitutes for the metallic currency into which they were convertible on demand. It arranged the foreign currency dealings necessary to finance British military operations abroad or to subsidize allies, and it handled the transactions in precious metals destined for the Royal Mint. It was also the main banker to the private sector— discounting bills of exchange and making short-term loans to joint stock companies on a scale which would have been outside the reach of a smaller or less privileged institution. By the end of the eighteenth century the Bank of England's note had become the most important liquid asset in the British monetary system.

In the latter decades of the eighteenth century it was generally recognized by those who operated in the money markets that substantial changes in the amount of money in circulation could be expected to have repercussions on the foreign exchange markets, reflected in outflows or inflows of bullion. Accordingly, in 1783, 1793, and again in 1797 the Bank temporarily restricted its loans to the private sector in order to stem an outflow of gold. Of course the outbreak of war in 1793, and the associated rise in government expenditure, greatly increased the dangers of crises of confidence setting off a rush to convert notes into gold and a drain on gold reserves which leaked either into internal hoards or abroad. For example, the combination of a war-induced inflation of prices, poor harvests in 1795 and 1796, and a fall in business confidence during 1797 precipitated by an invasion scare caused the Bank's reserves to plummet. Since the nation's gold reserves were crucial indicators of the credit-worthiness of a government at war the gold drain became a matter of urgent public interest; and in 1797 the Bank Restriction Act was passed. Designed originally to suspend convertibility of notes into cash until the crisis in confidence was over, it stayed in force for twenty-four years.

The Suspension of Cash Payments, as contemporaries called it, was equivalent to what twentieth-century governments were to call 'going off the Gold Standard'. Its effect was to break the link between the supply of money and the nation's reserves of precious metals and to change radically the rules of the game for the monetary authorities. The Bank could now expand the money supply without direct threat to its gold reserves. How much paper money came into circulation in these circumstances depended largely on government needs for war finance but partly on the judgement of the Bank's Directors as to the 'needs of trade'. The proper policy for the Bank to pursue became a matter of lively controversy. Those who took the orthodox traditional view (supported on the whole by *The Wealth of Nations*) argued that there was no reason for the Bank to worry about over-issue provided that it lent only to credit-worthy borrowers against the collateral of sound trade bills, that is, bills of exchange drawn in respect of sales of goods and services and due to be fully paid up in a matter of months. To the extent that the bulk of Bank lending was thus secured on 'real bills', or on the yield of specific taxes, this doctrine—the so-called real bills doctrine—provided plausible criteria for a prudent credit policy. Advances to the private sector could be viewed as a kind of revolving fund, having a turnover of a few months at the outside. In a credit system fed by this fast stream of regularly maturing bills, major commercial failures should have strictly localized effects on the money markets, provided that the lender of last resort remained unflustered by short-term aberrations in market confidence. Thus Henry Thornton, writing in the early nineteenth century, argued that the Bank had been over-hasty in restricting credit in 1783 and 1793 and that it could have contained these financial scares more efficiently by showing its willingness to go on steadily extending credit freely to credit-worthy borrowers. As events were to demonstrate, however, when the bulk of the banknotes issued were against unfunded borrowing for emergency war purposes, rather than against viable transactions in commercial goods and services, the real bills doctrine lost most of its force. The search for new theories of money and credit—more relevant to the complex, increasingly integrated, and changing institutions of the modern money market—then stimulated a lively debate inside and outside parliament.

The first systematic attempt to develop an up-to-date theory was made by Henry Thornton (1760–1815), a practising city banker and Member of Parliament who published in 1802 his *Enquiry into the Nature and Effects of the Paper Credit of Great Britain*. The book was written when the suspension of cash payments was still regarded as a temporary measure made necessary by a war which was unlikely to last much longer. There were indeed a few months of peace in 1802. It then seemed reasonable to associate the recent price inflation largely with non-monetary causes, such as two bad harvests in rapid succession and the high costs which war conditions imposed on the processes of trade. Accordingly, Thornton focused on the workings of a 'normal' monetary economy. He offered a balanced analysis of such questions as the relation between country bank note issues and the Bank's own note circulation, of the 'natural' limits to the money supply of a country on the gold standard, and of the factors governing the national and international distribution of the precious metals—an analysis which took into account the real as well as the monetary factors involved in the inflation process. The practical conclusion he drew from this analysis was that a well-informed monetary authority could best serve the public interest by tailoring its credit policies to sound 'needs of trade'.

Early in 1809, however, the debate on monetary policy flared up again when the exchange value of the pound sterling on the continental exchanges began to deteriorate alarmingly—as indicated by a widening gap between the Mint price of gold bullion and its international price. In August David Ricardo (1772–1823), then a practising stockbroker, joined the debate in a series of letters to the *Morning Chronicle*, later expanded into a pamphlet on *The High Price of Bullion, a Proof of the Depreciation of Banknotes* (1810). In 1810 a Select Committee of the House of Commons (including Thornton among its members) was appointed 'to enquire into the cause of the high price of gold bullion'.

Opinion in the debate polarized along two main lines of argument—then called bullionist and anti-bullionist. The bullionists, who included most of the leading economists of the day (even Thornton by this time), took the view that the recent deterioration in the value of the pound was largely attributable to an excess supply of Bank of England notes. Ricardo, for example, characteristically simplified the issue by ignoring all the non-monetary factors that might affect the value of money and adopting what twentieth-century commentators would describe as a pure monetarist perspective. 'Parliament,' he wrote, 'by restricting the Bank from paying in specie have enabled the conductors of that concern to increase or decrease at pleasure the quantity and amount of their notes; and the previous existing checks against an over-issue having been thereby removed, those conductors have acquired the power of increasing or decreasing the value of the paper money.' The banking and political establishment, by contrast, took the anti-bullionist view that there was no danger of an over-issue while the Bank lent only to credit-worthy borrowers. The Select Committee, however, followed Ricardo in concluding that the main cause of the depreciation of the currency had been an over-issue of paper money, and 'that this excess is to be ascribed to the want of a sufficient check and control in the issues of paper from the Bank of England; and originally the suspension of cash payments, which removed the natural and true control'. It finally recommended restoration of full convertibility of Bank notes into gold within two years—whether or not peace was restored in the interval. In the event, the political establishment remained unconvinced by the Committee's conclusions, and the fact that the value of the pound continued to fall from 1810 to 1813, although the Bank of England's note circulation rose hardly at all, seemed to invalidate the strict bullionist arguments. Full convertibility was not restored until 1821 and by then the general trend of prices was down rather than up.

In the 1820s the debate entered a new phase in which the opposing sides were taken by the members of the so-called Currency School on the one hand and the Banking School on the other. For even when the Bank of England was adopting an essentially bullionist policy, and government expenditures were contracting rather than expanding, the stability of the credit system was threatened by the fact that the country banks remained free to issue their own notes without formal restriction. In the speculative mania and financial crises of 1825, for example, domestic prices rose by 11 per cent in a single year— though, again, the Bank of England note circulation remained steady. The debate continued for a further two decades and was then finally settled by Peel's Bank Charter Act of 1844, which embodied the philosophy of the Currency School. The members of the Currency School took the Ricardian, hard monetarist, line and argued that a mixed currency ought to be operated in all essential respects as if it were a wholly metallic currency. The Banking School, on the other hand, followed Thornton in taking the view that, *given convertibility*, an over-issue of notes should be rapidly liquidated by natural market forces and that monetary stability could best be assured by giving the Bank discretion to adapt its credit policies to the needs of trade and to the short-term monetary factors affecting prices or exchange rates. Both schools of thought were agreed that the overriding objective of monetary policy was to maintain a stable value of money (a fixed gold price for the pound sterling in foreign as well as domestic markets). They differed, however, in their specification of the rules that ought to be laid down for the authorities when seeking to avoid the crises of confidence that might threaten this stability.

The solution that was written into the Bank Charter Act of 1844 was to centralize in the Bank of England primary responsibility for control of the nation's money supply (money being defined as metallic coin plus convertible bank notes). A maximum was set to the country bank notes issues and they were eventually to be absorbed by the Bank. The Bank's note issue was to be fully backed by gold apart from a fixed fiduciary issue covered by securities. The Act effectively determined until 1914—when the outbreak of the First World War again pushed the British economy off the gold standard—the institutional framework and rules of the game for British monetary policy. The rules were simple and readily intelligible to the business community at home and abroad. They were designed to insulate the central bank's monetary policy both from the narrow commercial interests of its directors and from the political interests of governments which might be tempted to finance increased public expenditure by debasing the currency.

In effect, the object of the Bank Charter Act was to establish the Bank of England as the nation's central monetary authority and at the same time to restrict its role in determining the money supply to the duty of automatically raising or lowering its discount rate in response to changes in the nation's bullion reserves. If gold flowed out of the country to finance a deficit on international account, the Bank was expected to raise its rate of discount by the amount necessary to force up the market rates of interest and thus attract a capital inflow (or discourage a capital outflow), so wiping out the deficit on the balance of payments. When a surplus on the balance of payments brought an inflow of gold, the appropriate policy was to lower the bank rate and so take advantage of the rise in gold reserves by expanding credit. When the balance of payments disequilibrium was due to temporary factors (such as a bad harvest, a trading partner at war, or a speculative mania on the stock exchange) the short-term movements of capital responding to a rise or fall in the bank rate would, it was supposed, be sufficient to correct the imbalance within a very few months. If the disequilibrium arose from more deep-seated changes in conditions of supply or demand (such as fundamental shifts in relative costs of production or in consumers' tastes), then contraction or expansion of the domestic credit supply as a result of interest rate changes would work through adjustments in domestic and international price levels to produce a lasting realignment of the balance of payments.

As it turned out, the seventy-year span over which the Bank Charter Act was in force (1844–1914) was a period of remarkable

monetary stability for the United Kingdom—and indeed for the
world economy generally in its later decades as one leading commercial country after another went to the gold standard. It was an
almost legendary stability which contrasted sharply with the variable experience of previous decades, and even more dramatically
with the post-1918 era when the international gold standard dis-
integrated and so-called 'hot money' reacted nervously and
unpredictably to frequent changes in economic and political circumstances by criss-crossing national boundaries in search of a
safe haven. How far the rules of the game laid down by the 1844
Act were responsible for preserving the golden-age stability that
vanished in 1914 is of course debatable. As far as the United
Kingdom was concerned, the fact that its overseas transactions
dominated the world's commodity markets, and also that London
was the undisputed financial centre of the world—so that British
balance of payments problems were not only uncommon but
typically short-lived—were no doubt crucial factors in maintaining a stable monetary environment. Rarely did bank rate have to
be held high long enough to depress appreciably domestic economic activity. Nor was the Act itself as inflexible in practice as
its originators intended or its critics complained. There were three
crisis years—1847, 1857, and 1866—when financial confidence
could be restored only by 'breaking the Banking Act', that is, by
resort to Government directive which temporarily waived the
legal limits on the fiduciary issue. Thereafter, the increased use of
cheques as a means of payment had the effect of circumventing
the rigid legal limits on the money supply and made it less and less
likely that financial crisis would require relaxation of those limits.
Moreover, in the hands of an increasingly experienced and
respected central bank, the rules of the game could be discreetly
manipulated in practice in ways that minimized money-market
shocks and uncertainties and that responded readily enough to
the needs of an expanding economy.

But perhaps the most important factor in the success of the
Bank's monetary policies over this period—success, that is, in
easily riding out financial crises and in maintaining a stable gold
value for the pound without hobbling the pace of economic
expansion—was that the philosophy embodied in the Bank

Charter Act fitted so comfortably with the ideological bias of the political establishment and the business community, as well as with orthodox political economy. In the last analysis it is the confidence of transactors that sustains the stability of the monetary system. The fact that the leading monetary authority in the financial centre of the world was formally committed to a policy stance which implied a minimum of discretionary action or arbitrary intervention in the money market gave ordinary decision-takers the confidence-inspiring impression that its behaviour pattern would match the moral as well as the rational expectations associated with the prevailing ideology of economic liberalism.

The third of the developments contributing to a transformation of the socio-economic problem situation facing policy-makers in the half century following publication of *The Wealth of Nations* was a marked acceleration in the process of industrialization. Before there had been major changes in the structure of national output, the industrial revolution had begun to disturb the traditional economic order of income distribution and to exacerbate the social upheaval involved in a major war and its aftermath. The problem rose to the surface of current political controversy towards the end of the war, mainly in relation to the debate on the Corn Laws, which were inflating the price of the nation's staple foodstuff by restricting imports of grain. It was Ricardo again who confronted the intellectual challenge by setting out systematically to fill the gaps and amend the conceptual confusions left by Adam Smith's theory of income distribution. There was by then a self-conscious intellectual community of political economists of whom several were committed to bring the principles of their young science to bear on the question of how agricultural protection affected the landlord's share in the national product. In 1815 three of them—Malthus, West, and Torrens—published pamphlets expounding a 'new theory of rent' which had emerged from their discussions. In the same year Ricardo—who made his reputation as a leading political economist in the debates on monetary policy, and his personal fortune on the Stock Exchange by acting as contractor for each of the government war loans issued during the years 1811–15— enlarged the scope of the debate and took it in more fruitful directions by publishing an *Essay on the Influence of a Low Price of Corn on the Profits of Stock*.

By 1814 Ricardo was already a substantial landowner himself, having acquired a 5,000-acre estate in Gloucestershire, including Gatcomb Park (which became his principal residence) and another large estate in Kent; and he continued to move his financial assets into land, so that by the time of his death in 1823 his total estate was estimated to be worth £700,000. From the end of the war, however, after making a spectacular 'killing' on the major war loan he negotiated four days before the battle of Waterloo, he devoted himself increasingly to his country estates, to writing on economics, and (from 1819) to speaking on economic issues in the House of Commons. As a source of inspiration to those engaged in the new 'science' of political economy his influence was second only to that of Adam Smith. Malthus, for example, his most persistent critic, indicated the quality of his standing among his fellow economists in the following tribute: 'I have so very high an opinion of Mr Ricardo's talent as a political economist, and so entire a conviction of his perfect sincerity and love of truth, that I frankly own I have sometimes felt almost staggered by his authority while I have remained unconvinced by his reasonings.'[2]

The *Essay on Profits* added a new dimension to the debate on income shares by relating it to a theory of economic growth in which profits—as the source of funds for capital investment—were treated as the strategic variable. Ricardo was then encouraged by his fellow economists, particularly by his friend James Mill, to expand the *Essay* into a book containing a full and general statement of his theoretical innovations. Now free from time-consuming stockbroking activities, he set himself the task of explaining the mechanism by which the 'produce of the earth—all that is derived from its surface by the united application of labour machinery and capital is divided among three classes of the community' (that is, landlords, capitalists and labourers) and of elucidating its implications for national economic growth. The resulting *Principles of Political Economy and Taxation* (1817), which went into a second and third edition, had a powerful impact on the methodology of orthodox political economy in the nineteenth century and is still a source of lively academic debate and reinterpretation in the late twentieth century.

There were two ways in which David Ricardo broke new ground in his approach to economic analysis. The first was in the sharpness of his focus on the *economy* as a distinct entity, not merely as a branch of society in general. His object was to formulate general laws or principles of economic behaviour, uncomplicated by reference to its historical, institutional, sociological, moral, or philosophical dimensions. The second lay in the determined consistency with which he applied an essentially mathematical technique of reasoning. Starting from a few strong, plausible, deliberately simplified initial assumptions, he formulated a set of relevant laws which could be synthesized into a coherent engine of thought designed to lead directly to decisive, unambiguous policy conclusions. Twentieth-century economists find it a familiar technique of analysis and recognize it as model building. The highly abstract, largely deductive, ahistorical and aphilosophical quality of Ricardo's economic methodology was unique at his time, as his contemporaries were well aware. J. R. McCulloch, for example, referred to the 'mathematical cast' of his reasoning. Malthus, whose *Principles of Political Economy* (1820) was written primarily as a critique of Ricardo's approach, began by insisting that: 'The science of political economy resembles more the science of morals and politics than the science of mathematics'; and then pinpointed his methodological objections to the Ricardian technique of analysis by complaining that: 'The principal cause of error, and of the differences which prevail at present among the scientific writers in political economy, appears to me to be a precipitate attempt to simplify and generalize.'[3]

Inevitably, it would seem, Ricardo's model-building technique led him into a radical reconstruction of the central theory of political economy—the theory of value. When he embarked on his research project designed to establish the 'correct principles' of income distribution and to draw the 'important deductions' concerning the level of national economic activity and its growth rate, he soon found it necessary to redefine and rework the Smithian conceptual framework relating to value and prices. He accepted the consensus view among political economists that the ultimate source of value or price was labour, but he recognized that to give dynamic force to that proposition it was necessary to define and measure the labour inputs in real rather than variable money terms. Adam Smith's interest in the theory of value had arisen in the context of an inquiry into 'the principles which regulate the exchangeable values of commodities in the market place' and he accordingly defined exchange value from the twin perspectives of demand and supply. On the one hand he argued that the 'only accurate measure of value' in a modern exchange economy where the 'division of labour has once thoroughly taken place' was the labour *commanded* by the relevant commodities in the market place. On the other (taking the supply point of view) he defined the real price of each commodity and of the national product as a whole as the sum of the wages, profits, and rents paid out to those involved in its creation.

For Ricardo this two-way perspective was evidence of muddled thinking on the part of Adam Smith. Having no interest in the essentially moral issues lying behind the attempts of Smith and his mercantilist predecessors to justify the prices at which commodities actually exchange in the market place, he had no use for a labour-commanded measure of value. On the other hand, he found Smith's supply-side definition—which reduced the values of commodities (and by aggregation the value of the national product as a whole) to the sum of profits, wages, and rents paid out in the production process—useless as a basis from which to deduce the mechanism relating income distribution and growth. For the implication of Smith's descriptive (rather than theoretical) cost-of-production account of the final value of output was that if, say, wage costs rose or fell, the price of output must be expected to rise or fall by an equivalent amount. In that case nothing could be inferred about the consequences for either profits or rent of a rise in wages. What Ricardo needed, if he was to use his model for predictive purposes, was a cost-of-production theory of value within which he could trace the dynamic relationship between factor shares. So in the first section of the first chapter of his *Principles* he set out to establish the principle that: 'The value of a commodity, or the quantity of any other commodity for which it will exchange, depends on the relative quantity of labour which is necessary for its production, and not on the greater or less compensation which is paid for the labour.' Starting from the twin assumptions derived from Adam Smith that capital investment was the key variable in the growth process and that profits were the basic source of funds for investment, he set out to develop a model of the economic system which could be used to analyse the effects of changes in factor shares on the national rate of economic growth.

Not surprisingly, in view of the particular policy issue which had sparked off his research in this area, and also in view of the fact that agriculture was still the premier industry of the modern capitalist economy, Ricardo developed his argument in terms of the conditions of agricultural production, using corn as the representative product. Characteristically he simplified his problems by reducing the number of variables in the cost-of-production = price equation. This was achieved by adopting the new theory of rent as developed by Malthus and others, which enabled him to eliminate rent from cost of production. So effectively did he expound this new theory that it is often referred to as the Ricardian theory of rent. What it said, in brief, was that the cost of production of corn varies with the fertility of the land and with its distance from the market, so that the price of corn has to be sufficient to cover the cost of production of the least productive piece of land in use—the marginal land, that is. On all but the marginal land, therefore, the cost of production of corn will fall short of its price, thus generating a surplus (or rent) which will accrue to the landlord if he cultivates the land directly or be extracted by him from a tenant if he lets it out. For Ricardo the implication of this theory was that rent does not enter into the cost of production of corn and so does not affect its price: in his own words, 'corn is not high because a rent is paid but a rent is paid because corn is high'.

With rents thus disposed of, Ricardo was able to discuss the causal connections between wages, profits, and value of output as a separate issue. He found an explanation of wages that was consistent with Malthus's doctrine of population—a subsistence theory of wages, that is—and he defined profit as the residual after paying out wages. In effect, he argued that the long-term supply price of labour, its 'natural' wage, was 'that price which is necessary to enable the labourers to subsist and perpetuate their race without either increase or diminution'. To this postulate Ricardo added a further assumption that was part of the prevailing consensus among political economists. It was that agriculture is subject to diminishing returns in the sense that as cultivation is extended or intensified, each additional input of effort into the production process tends to yield a decreasing increment of output. Or, to put it another way, as population expands and presses on increasingly scarce or less fertile land resources, the marginal productivity of labour falls and the wage cost involved in producing each extra bushel of corn rises, thus squeezing the surplus available for profits and reducing the annual rate of economic growth.

On the face of it, the package of assumptions and economic laws built into Ricardo's model yielded a very pessimistic prediction. It led inexorably to the stationary state, a situation of no growth which ensues when the combination of a rising population and fixed land resources drives up the cost of providing the subsistence wage, reduces profits to zero, and so chokes off the finance and incentive for new investment. To the modern political economist, conditioned by hindsight to expect a continuing process of productivity growth for a capitalist economy, this seems a strange conclusion and indeed it is not obvious that Ricardo envisaged the stationary state as altogether imminent. He made it clear, for example, that if something happened to raise the productivity of labour the squeeze on profits could be arrested and might even be reversed for a time. He may have laid less stress on the effects of technological progress in agriculture or of the introduction of labour-saving machinery than his twentieth-century counterpart would be inclined to do. But he added to the force of his onslaught on agricultural protection by developing a new and powerful theory of international trade which predicted that a country which had a comparative advantage in producing manufactured goods (as Britain certainly had) could postpone the advent of the stationary state for both itself and its trading partners by exporting those goods which it was best equipped to produce efficiently, and importing the primary products in which less developed countries had a comparative advantage. Characteristically, he drove home the macro-economic argument with a micro-economic illustration. 'Two men can both make shoes and hats, and one is superior to the other in both employments; but in making hats, he can only exceed his competitor by one-fifth or 20 per cent and in making shoes he can excel him by one-third or 33 per cent;—will it not be for the interest of both that the superior man should employ himself exclusively in making shoes and the inferior man in making hats?'

Ricardo's theory of international trade represented an important advance on Adam Smith's theory and provided the growing free trade lobby in Britain with an apparently irrefutable scientific case against all forms of protection. In essence the argument was that if each country specialized in the production of those commodities in which it had a comparative cost advantage, and imported items in which it was less efficient, world incomes generally would be maximized. More than that, to the extent that governments refrained from putting artificial barriers in the way of imports or exports, the pattern of world trade would conform 'naturally' to an optimum income-maximizing structure:

Under a system of perfectly free commerce, each country naturally devotes its capital and labour to such employments as are most beneficial to each. The pursuit of individual advantage is admirably connected with the universal good of the whole. By stimulating industry, by rewarding ingenuity and by using most efficaciously the peculiar powers bestowed by nature, it distributes labour most effectively and most economically: while by increasing the general mass of productions it diffuses general benefit, and binds together by one common tie of interest and intercourse, the universal society of nations throughout the civilized world.

In short, if all governments allowed the naturally self-regulating economic system to operate freely the advent of the stationary state could be postponed into the indefinite future.

Perhaps the most significant aspect of Ricardo's international trade theory, however, was that it was merely an extension of his corn model. The argument was not that by freeing commerce and increasing international trade, profits would rise in consequence of a widening of the extent of the market for domestic produce. It was that a fall in tariffs on, and hence in the prices of, those goods entering into the labourer's subsistence minimum would reduce the level of money wages, take the squeeze off profits, and thus promote capital accumulation and growth: 'If, instead of growing our own corn, or manufacturing the clothing and other necessaries of the labourer, we discover a new market from which we can supply ourselves with those commodities at a cheaper price, wages will fall and profits rise.' Implicit in the model was the Malthusian assumption that the natural tendency of population to grow would ensure a surplus of labour so that wages would naturally be forced down to subsistence levels. Explicit in the definition of profits as the residual after payment of wages and as the sole source of funds for capital accumulation was the notion of a tension between wages and profits which had to be resolved in favour of profits if capital accumulation was to be maintained at a growth-promoting level.

The overriding ideological conviction inspiring Ricardo's policy prescriptions and shaping his distinctive conceptual framework was an unshakeable belief in a causal link between economic liberty and economic progress. That was the hard core, the irrefutable assumption, underlying his vision of the economic system. It ensured that his general policy stance would be more *laissez-faire*, more completely opposed to direct government intervention in the economic system than, say, Adam Smith's. It also reflected the ideological spirit of his age, for nineteenth-century governments were becoming increasingly disinclined to maintain the expensive and often counter-productive apparatus of state control over prices or wages or industrial practices, while economic individualism played an important role in the thought-patterns of politicians and intellectuals for at least the first half of the nineteenth century. In this respect Ricardo reflected and gave 'scientific' support to an ideological bias which was already well entrenched in the mainstream of contemporary economic ideas.

More interesting, however, is the legacy bequeathed to a less orthodox stream of ideas by the class conflicts inherent in Ricardo's own model of the modern capitalist economy. From his theory of rent he had deduced that all except the landlords would be injured by an increase in the price of corn and that 'the interest of the landlord is always opposed to that of the consumer and manufacturer'. But he rejected the charge that he was the enemy of the landlords. He would no doubt have been equally affronted had he known that Karl Marx would use his labour theory of value in conjunction with his surplus theory of profits as the basis for an exploitation theory of wages. For questions of justice had no place in Ricardo's economic model. There were no ethical judgments attached, for example, to the following bland account of the productive process: 'Each year the capitalist begins his operations, by having food and necessaries in his possession of the value of £13,000, all of which he sells in the course of the year to his own workmen for that sum of money and during the same period, he pays the like amount of money for wages: at the end of the year they replace in his possession food and necessaries of the value of £15,000, £2000 of which he consumes himself, or disposes of as may best suit his pleasure and gratification.'[4] Nor, when he referred to the constant competition of machinery and labour, or when he drew the conclusion that 'the opinion entertained by the labouring class, that the employment of machinery is frequently detrimental to their interests, is not founded on prejudice and error, but is conformable to the correct principles of political economy',[5] was he aware of having provided ammunition for the anti-machine lobby of radical writers or of having justified the machine breakers. On the contrary, he insisted that any attempt on the part of the State to discourage the use of machinery in domestic production would drive capital abroad and further add to the technological unemployment stemming from the adoption of labour-saving machinery.

It has to be admitted, however, that the debate on the machinery question was at a very early stage when Ricardo died in 1823 at the age of 51. The industrial revolution was evidently well under way, but it had not yet had massive effects on the nation's industrial structure, rate of economic growth and average living standards. In common with most contemporary political economists who discussed capital as a factor of production, Ricardo thought of it primarily as circulating capital rather than fixed capital, and hence as a factor that was complementary to rather than competitive with labour. The only fully-fledged factory industry was cotton spinning (power weaving was still at an experimental stage); the iron industry was only just starting to recover from its post-war depression; the official value of exports from the United Kingdom had not yet regained its 1815 level; and the railway age did not begin until 1830. In essence, then, Ricardo's *Principles of Political Economy and Taxation* reflected the problems of a pre-industrial rather than an indus-trialized capitalism, and the brief chapter on 'the influence of machinery on the interests of the different classes of society', which he appended to the third edition, published in 1821, was not fully integrated with the rest of that book.

6

The search for a scientific consensus

> With respect to Political Economy, the period of contro-
> versy is passing away, and that of unanimity is rapidly
> approaching. Twenty years hence there will scarcely exist
> a doubt respecting any of its fundamental principles.
>
> Robert Torrens, 1821

> In matters of philosophy and science authority has ever
> been the great opponent of truth. A despotic calm is
> usually the triumph of error. In the republic of the
> sciences sedition and even anarchy are beneficial in the
> long run to the greatest happiness of the greatest number.
>
> W. S. Jevons, *Theory of Political Economy*, 1871

By the 1830s there existed in England an active, self-conscious intellectual community dedicated to pursuing a scientific political economy. The community had effectively identified itself in 1821 by founding a Political Economy Club which met regularly in London through the rest of the nineteenth century. Its elected membership included—in addition to various leading parlia-mentarians—bankers, merchants, civil servants, journalists, Royal Society Fellows, and professors of political economy, a majority indeed of the individuals who could speak with author-ity on some aspect or another of economic affairs. The shared commitment bringing them together was a readiness to debate currently urgent economic policy problems within a disciplined analytical framework; and they acknowledged an objective (if as yet incomplete) system of economic laws. In the early years of the Club its members brought to it a wide range of practical experi-ence and scholarship which helped to buttress a remarkable degree of unanimity on the basic premises and philosophy of their discipline. They thus represented a distinctive school of economic thought, which—though far from monolithic in its opinions and policy prescriptions—accepted Adam Smith's vision of the 'natural' economic system as their point of departure, Bentham's rules for private and public decision-taking as their criteria for economic legislation, and Ricardo as their most admired exponent of scientific analysis.

The Benthamite inheritance was significant not only in giving a characteristic slant to the shared ideological preconceptions of English classical political economy, but also in relation to the future ideology of their discipline. What the classical economists got from Jeremy Bentham (1748–1832) was not an addition to their conceptual or theoretical equipment, for his grasp of the way the economic system worked was short both on perception and cogency. He did, however, fill an important gap in Adam Smith's version of the 'science of a statesman or legislator' by responding directly to the ethical problems raised by socio-economic conflicts inherent in a developing industrial revolution. Unemployment and poverty were not new problems, but they had always tended to produce more acute social distress and unrest in an urban environment (where economic relations between individuals tend to be relatively impersonal and competitive) than in the traditional settled village community. So when the rise of agrarian and industrial capitalism accelerated the pace of urbanization and subjected an increasing proportion of the labour force to unpredictable shifts in social status and income distribution, the need to find new ways of maintaining social cohesion became urgent. Essentially it was a question of establishing agreed criteria of social justice for a changing economy in which neither custom nor religion seemed to provide clear moral imperatives. What Bentham offered the policy-maker was a normative perspective on economic behaviour, a mechanical working rule to guide legislators faced with choices between alternative policy options, and an analytical technique which dealt with moral issues on apparently objective or scientific, rather than on subjective or intuitive, grounds.

Bentham started from the simplistic premise that the economic motives of individuals were fundamentally egoistic, indeed hedonistic, and could be reduced to a wholly rational propensity to maximize pleasure and minimize pain. His most influential work, for example, *The Principles of Morals and Legislation* (1789), postulated that: 'Nature has placed mankind under the guidance of two sovereign masters, "pain" and "pleasure". It is for them alone to point out what we ought to do, as well as to determine what we shall do. On the one hand the standard of right and wrong, on the other the chain of causes and effects are fastened to their throne.' From this axiomatic starting point he developed the notion of a 'felicific calculus' whereby rational individuals could be presumed to assess the personal utility of their economic transactions, and governments could (and by implication should) design the institutions and the statutes which would induce their subjects to behave in ways that were least injurious to other members of the community.

The simple piece of 'moral arithmetic' which gave the impartial legislator his objective working rule was that 'it is the greatest happiness of the greatest number that is the measure of right or wrong'. Implicit in this bland, apparently unambiguous moral rule, however, was a package of questionable assumptions: in particular, that it was in principle possible to measure the total utility (which Bentham equated to happiness) not only of the individual, but also of the nation; and that qualitative differences between utilities (governed by personal tastes or needs) should be ignored in adding them together—'quantum of pleasure being equal', insisted Bentham confidently, 'pushpin is as good as poetry'. Also implicit in his assumptions was that rational behaviour is equivalent to moral behaviour—whether on the part of individuals or of the State.

Not all classical economists swallowed Bentham's utilitarian philosophy at its full hedonistic strength and none of them made use of his concept of measurable utility—an idea which was to be revived by later generations of economists. The Ricardian generation proved highly receptive to the greatest happiness principle, however, for a number of reasons. As disciples of Adam Smith, they defined the political economist's role as one of offering scientifically informed, distinterested advice to legislators intent on promoting national economic growth. As followers of Ricardo, they accepted a model of economic growth which hinged on the distribution of rewards between factors of production and nominated profits as the accelerator in the growth process. The Ricardian model in effect pointed up more sharply than Smith had ever done the inherent conflicts of interest between factors of production in a growing economy. For, on the one hand it demonstrated that the interests of landowners were at war with those of all other classes in the community—a conclusion of some importance in a State where the balance of economic power favoured the aristocracy and gentry; on the other hand it revealed an apparent conflict of interest between capital and labour. In Ricardo's scenario, for example, a rise in the labourers's share of national product (unaccompanied by a corresponding rise in labour productivity) must reduce the share of profits which funded the annual new investment necessary for the maintenance of long-term growth. In an increasingly secular, libertarian, acquisitive, and changing society, Bentham's normative rule that the object of all legislation should be the greatest happiness of the greatest number offered the classical economists a seductively simple rule of thumb which could be used to justify tough growth-promoting policies without reference to outdated principles of morality or economic justice.

Once the Napoleonic Wars were over, a host of disturbing socio-economic problems associated with post-war structural change and continuing industrial revolution rose to the top of government agenda. Acceleration in the rate of population growth (and especially of urbanization) combined with the disequilibrating effects of industrial fluctuations and technological change to create deep pockets of economic distress and an endemic tendency to local riots. It was an era in which the trend in public opinion favoured a decrease rather than an increase in central government intervention in the economy; but the need to prevent localized unrest from exploding into the revolutionary upheavals then familiar events in continental Europe seemed to require the exercise of more rational foresight at the national policy-making level than ever before. So, although the classical economists had lost none of their faith in the growth-promoting virtues of a freely competitive economic system, they were beginning to realize that Adam Smith's invisible hand was not by itself sufficient to maintain social harmony in an economy subject to constant and unpredictable change in the level and distribution of incomes.

To pragmatic applied economists, concerned to formulate policy prescriptions that would serve the public interest as a whole, the greatest happiness principle offered a generally acceptable moral imperative, which could be used both to override the bias of the privileged minority currently dominating Parliament and to bypass the ethical dilemmas posed by conflicts between economic and social objectives—for example between national economic growth and a humane distribution of incomes. A number of the members of the Political Economy Club were directly involved in the legislative process themselves. In Parliament they spearheaded the attack on the Corn Laws, were unanimous in advocating the need to minimize government expenditures *and* taxes (at local as well as national levels), and exerted a persistent pressure in favour of free trade. Most of them were also supporters of electoral reform and held Malthusian views on population growth—although there was less agreement on how to contain the demographic devil.

Theorists who were alive to the moral and logical foundations of their discipline, however, found the simplistic utilitarian philosophy less than satisfactory. This was particularly so for scholars such as J.S. Mill and Karl Marx, who pursued their economic enquiries against a broad background of social and philosophical studies and who were well tuned in to modern cultural trends and influences. A vigorous reaction against the extreme rationalism of the Enlightenment era, for example, had already set in by the end of the eighteenth century among the philosophers and littérateurs who were shaping educated opinion. Romantic and nationalist ideas being developed in Germany spread across most of western Europe in the early nineteenth-century. In this more sentimental climate, classical political economy was open to the charge of being founded on barbaric and inhumane social values for example, because it (1) exalted motives of personal economic gain; (2) depended increasingly on would-be precise, essentially mathematical (hence amoral or ahistorical) techniques of analysis; and (3) opposed policies designed to redistribute incomes from rich to poor as a recipe for population explosion and economic decline. It was the Romanticists who launched the most withering condemnations. Among them, Samuel Taylor Coleridge was probably the most wounding of critics, not because he fancied himself as an economist (according to Thomas De Quincey, Coleridge 'fancied he had made discoveries in the science and even promised us a systematic work on the subject'), but because the 'sage of Highgate' had such a reverential following among the educated élite.

In England it was John Stuart Mill (1806–73) who effectively absorbed the weight of the Romantic onslaught on Ricardian political economy and justified the hard core of economic liberalism in epistemological, philosophical, and political terms. Mill, who in 1838 described Bentham and Coleridge as 'the two great seminal minds of their age', was to achieve greater prophetic weight himself than either, for he was the great synthesizer. He had come under the influence of Bentham, a friend of his father's, when a mere infant. James Mill, also a political economist, a close friend of Ricardo, and a formidable personality in his own right, shared with Bentham the view that it was vital to develop his young son's intellectual potential by subjecting him to an intensive process of formal education from the earliest possible age. He taught the boy himself. John Stuart was learning Greek at the age of 3, grappling with calculus at 11, and studying Ricardo's recently published *Principles of Political Economy* at 13. A year spent in France at the home of Bentham's brother, Samuel, gave the lad a first-hand and lasting intimacy with continental liberalism. By the time he was 15, and back in England, he was put to the task of editing Bentham's *Rationale of Judicial Evidence* and succeeded in producing a coherent five-volume work out of a mountain of highly technical manuscripts.

Mill's *Autobiography*, drafted in 1853–4, described the turning point in his intellectual development which occurred in his late teens when he began to take a grip on Bentham's utilitarian doctrine: 'I now had opinions, a creed, a doctrine, a philosophy; in one, among the best senses of the word, a religion, the inculcation of which could be made the principal outward purpose of a life.' Still in his teens, still under the influence of his father, he set up a debating society (dubbed by him the Utilitarian

Society), gathering round him a group of eager students whom he described later as 'the first propagators of what was afterwards called "philosophical radicalism" '. Their main shared conviction, apart from their commitment to Benthamite utilitarianism and Ricardian economic theory, was Malthus's population principle: 'This great doctrine', wrote Mill, 'originally brought forward as an argument against an indefinite improvability of human affairs, we took up with ardent zeal in the contrary sense, as indicating the sole means of realizing that improvability by securing full employment at high wages to the whole labouring population through a voluntary restriction of the increase of their numbers.' They also shared 'an almost unbounded confidence in the efficacy of two things: representative government, and complete freedom of discussion', together with a profound distaste for aristocratic rule and ecclesiastical dogma. In sum they shared the political ideology which coloured Mill's thinking to the end of his life.

Not surprisingly perhaps, after this hothouse educational process, this early exposure to such powerful adult personalities and to the extensive and intensive programme of reading and debating into which he was so forcefully propelled from childhood, Mill had a nervous breakdown in his twenty-first year. He was than a junior clerk in the East India company—a job found for him by his father in 1823 and in which he rose steadily to a post equivalent to that of a secretary of state before retiring in 1858. Significantly, his description in the *Autobiography* of his mental crisis is studded with poetical passages from Coleridge, for that was when Mill began to identify the inadequacies of the utilitarian doctrine. He now recognized the element of truth in the Romantics' description of a Benthamite 'as a mere reasoning machine', of 'political economy as hard-hearted' and of the ultilitarian approach as 'cold calculation'. In the long struggle out of confused depression he found himself increasingly appreciative of romantic poetry and music, read Carlyle, Coleridge, and Goethe with deepening sympathy, and found friends amongst his former antagonists in debate—for instance, Christian socialists such as F. D. Maurice and John Sterling. Mill was the last of the English philosopher-economists, the polymaths (in the tradition of Smith and Bentham) whose researches ranged over a wide area of moral and social sciences and for whom political economy was the most highly developed, but never the most important, branch of the study of society. He had written several articles and essays on economics in the 1820s and 1830s, but his early pieces—later collected for publication under the title *Essays on Some Unsettled Questions of Political Economy* (1844)—were largely focused on epistemological and method-ological issues. They were part of the research programme which led up to his first major work, published when he was 37, and entitled *A System of Logic, Ratiocinative and Inductive: Being a connected view of the principles of evidence and the methods of scientific investigation* (1843). Mill's *Logic*, his most important and carefully researched book, provided the analytical framework for his other influential monographs on political economy, utilitarianism, liberty, representative government, and the sub-jection of women. It went into eight editions during his lifetime (including a cheap edition aimed at working class readership) and rapidly became the Bible of the liberal intellectuals. They revered it for its erudition, its eclecticism, its open-mindedness, and its dedication to the idea of free thought as the key to the perfect-ibility of human nature and social institutions.

For economists, the importance of *A System of Logic* lay in its strong claims for the scientific basis of social science. Mill argued, for example, that human behaviour is as explicable in terms of natural laws (or rather tendencies, since all scientific laws are conditional) as are the phenomena studied by physical scientists. Economists could take comfort, for example, from such observations as: '. . . in the sciences which deal with phenomena in which artificial experiments are impossible (as in the case of astronomy) or in which they have a very limited range (as in mental philosophy, social science and even physiology) induction from direct experience is practised at a disadvantage in many cases equivalent to impracticability; from which it follows that the methods of those sciences, in order to accomplish any-thing worthy of attainment, must be to a great extent, if not principally, deductive.'[1] Mill gave political economy formal identity as a science by defining its subject matter as 'the class of social phenomena in which the immediately determining causes are principally those which act through the desire of wealth; and in which the psychological law mainly concerned is the familiar one that a greater gain is preferred to a smaller'.[2] He then went on to disarm the critics who attacked the spurious universality of economic laws by admitting frankly that many of the laws of political economy 'are only locally true': for example, 'empirical laws of human nature which are tacitly assumed by English thinkers are calculated only for Great Britain and the United States. Among other things, an intensity of competition is constantly supposed which, as a general mercantile fact, exists in no country in the world except those two.'[3]

Most important of all, perhaps, Mill modified and put into scientific perspective the 'interest-philosophy of the Bentham school' (which Carlyle and others had raged against as a 'pig-philosophy'), by interpreting it as a convenient abstraction relevant only to the worldly interests of a majority of mankind, and by calling it 'the most remarkable example afforded by our own times of the geometrical method in politics; emanating from persons who are well aware of the distinction between science and art'. He had already, in 1831, written an essay (extensively reproduced in his *Logic*) making the point that the science of political economy is essentially an *abstract* science, reasoning on the basis of 'hypotheses strictly analogous to those which under the name of definitions are the foundation of the other abstract sciences'. Its starting assumption that economic man is solely concerned with acquiring and consuming wealth was simply a necessary abstraction, as arbitrary but as justifiable as the geometer's definition of a line as 'that which has length but not breadth'; not, he added, 'that any political economist was ever so absurd as to suppose that mankind are really so constituted, but because this is the mode in which science must necessarily proceed. When an effect depends upon a concurrence of causes, those causes must be studied one at a time.'[4] However, as Mill was careful to point out, the problem with political economy, as indeed with the moral sciences in general, is that precisely defined boundaries between related disciplines may turn out to be inapplicable in practice. Where the causes and consequences of human behaviour spill across disciplines 'the mere political economist, he who has studied no science but Political Economy, if he attempt to apply his science to practice will fail'.

Mill's *System of Logic* was the end-result of more than a decade of research aimed at developing a set of principles of scientific method which were as relevant to the study of human society as to the investigation of the physical world. His *Principles of Political Economy with some of their Applications to Social Philosophy* (1848) involved application of that methodology to the branch of social science which he believed to be the most mature. Completed in roughly two years, it was designed to update Smith's *Wealth of Nations* by expounding the current received doctrine of political economy (mainly based on Ricardo's *Principles*, with which Mill had begun his study of the subject in 1819) and by relating it more explicitly than any of his predecessors had done to a modern philosophy of society. Mill had no intention of revising the existing corpus of economic theory, though, as later historians of economic thought have shown, he did actually introduce various original extensions and modifications of its conceptual and analytical apparatus which had lasting significance. The major difference between his book and Ricardo's, however, lay not in theoretical content but in scope and method. Mill's *Principles* was more eclectic in its use of economic theory, more discursive and less mathematically consistent in exposition, more sophisticated in its epistemological foundations, more imaginative in its perception of the social and ideological implications of alternative economic policies, and more accessible to the intelligent general reader.

It was a corollary of Mill's broader perspective on economic analysis that he never lost sight of the fact that pure economic theory is severely limited in its relevance to actual social or economic situations and that it needs to be supplemented by non-economic as well as economic data before it can be usefully applied to the analysis of actual problems or events. He went on, for example, to draw a distinction between the laws of production which 'partake of the nature of physical truths' and the laws of distribution which, being largely determined by social attitudes and institutions, could in principle be altered by purposive collective decisions. This enabled him to discuss the pros and cons of 'different modes of distributing the produce of land and labour, which have been adopted in practice or may be conceived in theory' in terms of comparative advantage rather than in ideological terms, and to discuss judiciously and open-mindedly various forms of socialism, say, or the contrast between a custom-dominated society and market economy where the rules of the game are set by competition.

Mill's *Principles*, published two years after the repeal of the Corn Laws, had demolished the last major obstacle to complete free trade in Britain, replaced Ricardo's *Principles* as the author-itative textbook of English classical political economy. It was the book with which Marshall began his study of economics in the 1860s and it remained the leading introductory text for serious academic readers in North America as well as the United Kingdom until the early years of the twentieth century. Additionally it spawned various derivative texts designed to popularize its message for the general reader or to provide the ordinary under-graduate with a crammer, for instance, Henry Fawcett's *Manual of Political Economy* (1863). Its enduring success may be attributed largely to its faithful reflection of the ethos of late nineteenth-century liberalism, its systematically argued defence of the dismal science against accusations of inhumanity or excess-ive abstraction, and its optimistic vision of the prospects for economic development. Where the Ricardian model of economic growth indicated an inherent conflict between capital and labour and led inexorably to the prospect of a stationary state, Mill's faith in human perfectibility suggested that the stationary state did not necessarily imply 'that the stream of human industry should finally spread itself into an apparently stagnant sea'. On the contrary, 'when in addition to just institutions the increase of mankind shall be under the deliberate guidance of judicious fore-sight' each rise in output per head could help to reduce the drudgery of the majority and become 'the means of improving and elevating the universal lot'. In the booming 1850s and 1860s, when the volume of international trade was expanding at an unprecedented rate—stimulated by a worldwide dismantling of tariff barriers and lubricated by the gold discoveries in the United

States and Australia—such optimistic forecasts touched the spirit of a new age in Britain.

The Great Victorian Boom indeed gave a special boost to the public reputation of political economists whose persistent advocacy of free trade had been so evidently justified by events. It ensured that the strong claims for the validity of economic theory that were made in Mill's *Principles* would be read in a credulous climate. If economists displayed less of the 'imposing unanimity' on which textbook writers in the physical sciences could depend, the reader must suppose from Mill's account that their valid disagreements were confined to the interface between theoretical and applied economics. For it was there, he suggested, that the complexities and uncertainties of changing actual situations made it particularly difficult to identify and allow for the exceptions to economic laws; and it was at this frontier that new research was most urgently needed. Fortunately—according to Mill—pure economic theory had already established a sufficient basis of scientific certainty to provide the framework for a progressive research programme in applied economics: 'Happily,' he wrote in his *Principles*, 'there is nothing in the laws of value which remains for the present or any future writer to clear up; the theory of the subject is complete.' This bold assertion was to lend a certain poignancy to his personal recantation, two decades later, of one of the laws commonly deduced from orthodox Ricardian value theory—the wage-fund doctrine. That, as stated in its most widely accepted form in 1865 by Mill's popularizer, Henry Fawcett (then occupying the Cambridge chair of political economy), ran thus:

The circulating capital of a country is its wage-fund. Hence, if we desire to calculate the average money wage received by each labourer, we simply have to divide the amount of capital by the number of the labouring population. It is therefore evident that the average money wage cannot be increased until either the circulating capital is augmented or the number of the labouring population is diminished.

The attraction of the wage-fund doctrine for the principal beneficiaries of the Great Victorian Boom (whether as capitalist entrepreneurs, or as middle-class professionals and rentiers, or as artisans whose skill was in scarce supply) was that it effectively justified an inequitable distribution of incomes on essentially amoral grounds. It offered a scientific law asserting that this year's increase in the labourer's share of national product must be at the expense of the profits and interest required to supply the circulating capital on which next year's national income has to depend. The obvious corollary was that the efforts of trade unions to raise wage rates were doomed to be counter-productive. As Mill put it himself in his *Principles*: '. . . if they aimed at obtaining higher wages than the rate fixed by demand and supply—the rate which distributes the whole working capital of the country among the entire working population—this could only be accomplished by keeping a part of their number permanently out of employment.' Significantly, moreover, although Mill was moved to admit in an article in the *Fortnightly Review* (1869) that 'There is no law of nature making it inherently impossible for wages to rise to the point of absorbing not only the funds which he [the capitalist] had intended to devote to carrying on his business, but the whole of what he allows for his private expenses, beyond the necessaries of life', he failed to carry this recantation through to his textbook. The modest amendment introduced into his last (1871) edition continued to insist that trade unions had a strictly limited scope for raising the general level of wages at the expense of profits—beyond these limits the increase in wage costs would lead to increased unemployment.

Meanwhile, a consensus that the fundamental theories and laws of political economy must be detached from moral principles and value judgments was steadily gathering strength among leading economic theorists during the nineteenth century. There were those who were unable to absolve scientific political economy from ethical considerations, however. Among them, probably the most influential was Karl Marx (1818–83) whose analysis of the way the modern industrial economy operated was simultaneously a moral indictment of its monumental injustices. In 1848, the same year as Mill published the first edition of his *Principles*, Marx and Engels collaborated to launch the Communist Manifesto on a revolution-torn Europe. This document, commissioned by the Communist League (formed in London in

1847—the successor to a secret League of the Just which German socialists had set up in Paris in 1836), was designed to incite the revolution of the proletariat by explaining its inevitability. In so doing, the Communist Manifesto presented an imaginative vision of the contemporary economic problem situation through the medium of: (1) an analysis of the stages of economic development, leading up to the currently highly productive system of large scale competitive modern industry; (2) identification of its dynamic and exploitative characteristics; (3) a condemnation of the oppressive regime imposed by the property-owning bourgeoisie on the working classes; and (4) a rousing call for revolutionary action on a global scale by those 'who have nothing to lose but their chains. They have a world to win.'

The Marxian world-view was distinguished by its moralizing passion and its deterministic prognosis. Its prophetic message rolled out of the Manifesto in a series of dramatic tableaus—for example, 'The bourgeoisie during its rule of scarce one hundred years has created more massive and more colossal productive forces than have all preceding generations together. Subjection of nature's forces to man, machinery, application of chemistry to industry and agriculture, steam-navigation,. railways, electric telegraphs, clearing of whole continents for cultivation, canalization of rivers, whole populations conjured out of the ground—what earlier century had even a presentiment that such productive forces slumbered in the lap of social labour?'

But a system of production based on exploitation of the proletarian majority and cut-throat competition amongst the capitalist minority must be inherently unstable: 'The development of Modern Industry therefore cuts from under its feet the very foundation on which the bourgeoisie produces and appropriates products. What the bourgeoisie produces, above all, is its own grave diggers. Its fall and victory of the proletariat are equally inevitable.'

The vision, however, came first and the task of establishing its scientific validity became Marx's life work. He spent the next three and a half decades building the socio-economic model which would 'lay bare the law of motion of modern society'. After getting his doctorate in Greek philosophy from the University of

Berlin in 1841, he had effectively spiked his personal ambitions for an academic career by writing anti-authoritarian articles for the press. Then in 1849, after his adventures in radical journalism had led to his expulsion from France, Belgium, and Germany, he took up residence in London and began a study in depth of what he called 'the confounded ramifications of political economy'. The first monograph to emerge from this programme was *A Contribution to a Critique of Political Economy*, first published (in Germany) in 1859 and translated into English in 1904. That was a prelude to his masterpiece, *Capital: a Critique of Political Economy* (volume I, 1867 in German, and in English posthumously in 1887). Only the first volume appeared in his lifetime; volumes II (1885) and III (1894) were edited and put into the press by his friend and collaborator Frederic Engels and were not translated into English until the early twentieth century. Marx also wrote, in the early 1860s, a history of economic thought which he intended to publish as volume IV of *Capital* but which did not in fact appear in print until 1905–10 as *Theories of Surplus Value* (in German); it was more than fifty years later that this became available in English translation. Thus, although Marx pursued his research programme in political economy in England—using the rich resources of the British Museum library—his theorizing had no direct impact on English-speaking economists either in Britain or in the United States until well into the twentieth-century.

On the other hand, he was himself directly and explicitly inspired by English classical political economy. 'We have proceeded from the premises of political economy. We have accepted its language and its laws', he wrote in 1844. But he was selective in his borrowings. He shared its presumption that the system within which individual producers co-operated to earn their livelihood was governed by laws that operated as independently of human volition as did the laws which natural scientists found applicable to the physical universe; and he was particularly responsive (more so than most mainstream English economists) to two of its lessons: (1) Adam Smith's historical perspective on the way the modern system of production had developed on the strength of the institution of private property—especially private ownership of the capital resources which were the key to economic growth; and (2) Ricardo's focus on the conflict between capital and labour. On the other hand, he was highly critical of the gaps in the explanatory power of orthodox political economy—in particular of its failure to fulfil its scientific function of demonstrating the mechanism by which each stage in economic development led inexorably to the next. That was the gap that he set out to fill.

Three things ensured that Marx's approach to the reconstruction of political economy would set him on a divergent track from that of mainstream English economics. The first was the fact that his continental education had given him a philosophical background of ideas and analytical techniques that were quite foreign to his English counterparts—even to the highly-educated J.S. Mill. The second was that his interest in economics was stimulated by a different ideology—primarily by a raging sense of the injustice associated with the modern, capitalistic, system of economic organization. The third was a matter of personal temperament rather than of education or perception of reality or moral values; it was that he was always an aggressive seeker after scientific truth (as well as social justice), never the dispassionate observer.

The teacher whose ideas were most influential in shaping Marx's distinctive economic methodology was Hegel, who had held the chair of philosophy at the University of Berlin from 1818 until he died in 1831 and dominated its debates in political philosophy for a great deal longer. From Hegel, Marx acquired the dialectical technique of analysis which underpinned his vision of a development process arising out of a progressive sequence of conflicts and revolutions. Hegel had depicted the development of human knowledge as a succession of conflicts between opposing ideas—thesis provoking antithesis and the solution (synthesis) embodying the best of both. This was the analogy on which Marx based his explanation of the historical evolution of the economic system. According to his own account (in the preface to his *Contribution to a Critique of Political Economy*), his critical study of the Hegelian philosophy of law took him to the conclusion 'that neither legal relations nor political forms could be comprehended . . . on the basis of a so-called general development of the human mind, but that on the contrary they originated in the material conditions of life, the totality of which Hegel, following the example of English and French thinkers of the eighteenth century, embraces within the term "civil society"; that the anatomy of this civil society, however, has to be sought in political economy'.[5]

Characteristically, then, Marx transposed the teaching of his mentors in philosophy or politics (as in economics) into a format and set of conclusions which bore little relation to the message intended by their originators. Whereas the Hegelian dialectic, for example, explained a logically inevitable progress arising out of conflicting ideas, Marx applied the same deterministic techniques to analyse a chronological sequence of stages in the development of successive modes of production, each stage carrying the seeds of class conflict which would destroy it. Similarly, whereas Hegel saw history as political history and identified the Prussian monarchical state as the culminating form of civil society in which all men are free, Marx focused on economic history and identified the goal of absolute freedom with a communist society in which all producers participate equally and where there is thus no need for the exercise of State authority to maintain social order.

It was an essentially similar inversion of perspective that allowed Marx to build an exploitation theory of profits on the same foundation stones as those on which the classical economists had based their iron law of wages. Ricardo, for example, had explained (*a*) the value of output as a function of the quantity of labour embodied in the production process; (*b*) the wage cost of output as dependent on the subsistence requirements of the labour force; and (*c*) profits as the residual after subtracting the wage bill from the sales value of output. A small but crucial shift in point of view was sufficient to enable Marx to deduce from this set of propositions that if the labourer's product is sold by the employer at its full value, and the labourer is paid only the value of his subsistence needs, then the surplus appropriated by the capitalist employer measures the extent to which the labour force is exploited by the system. This theory of surplus value played a strategic role in Marx's dynamic model, being used by him as evidence both for the intolerable injustice of the system and for the inevitability of revolution. After citing, for example, Mill's famous doubt whether 'all the mechanical inventions yet made have lightened the day's toil of any human being', Marx commented scornfully: 'That is however by no means the aim of the capitalistic application of machinery. Like every other increase in the productiveness of labour, machinery is intended to cheapen commodities, and by shortening that portion of the working-day in which the labourer works for himself, to lengthen the other portion that he gives without an equivalent to the capitalist. In short it is a means for producing surplus-value.'[6] The contrast between Marx's doctrine of surplus value and the classical wage fund doctrine—both based on essentially the same economic laws—is instructive as well as striking. For there was one premise that mainstream political economy tacitly took for granted and Marx explicitly rejected—the assumption that the capitalist mode of production was fixed for the foreseeable future. It was a crucial difference between the two competing systems of economic thought that developed over the following century.

Much of the success of the philosopher-economists, such as Smith and Mill, in winning over the minds of their contemporaries and successors lay in the confident breadth and depth of their vision. Marx's economic ideas were also grounded in a coherent general framework of ideas—philosophical, social, political, and historical as well as economic. But whereas the philosophical preconceptions that Adam Smith bequeathed to his classical followers included the premise that economic progress emerges *naturally* out of a God-given harmony of individual sentiments and egotistical motives, Marx had inherited Hegel's assumption of a rational universe in which progress in human wisdom evolves out of a sequence of logical conflicts and revolutions. He also inherited from Hegel a more organic, less atomistic, vision of modern society than was typical of the English tradition of political philosophy with its strongly individualistic orientation.

Accordingly, in adapting Hegel's dialectic analysis to his unique brand of historical materialism (in which *economic* factors dominated in explaining the anatomy and long-term development of civil society) Marx located the critical conflicts *not* in the competition between self-interested individuals and enterprises pursuing micro-economic gains in the market-place, but between social classes struggling for political control over the productive resources on which their share in the gross national product hinged. In so doing, he brought a distinctive social (as well as political) dimension into his system of economic theory. Meanwhile, and in sharp contrast, leading classical economists were tending increasingly to associate the scientific content of their discipline with 'pure' economic theory.

By including social and political variables in his model of economic development, Marx found a way of introducing dynamic properties that could not be accommodated in more rigorously conceived models. Taking his cue from Ricardo, for example, and accepting the capital-labour relationship as the strategic element in the current economic situation, he went much further by identifying it as the key to the past and future development of modern economic society. For Marx, that is to say, the separation of producers into two classes—those owning the means of the production and those supplying the necessary labour power—had established the social and institutional framework which enabled modern capitalist industry to generate unprecedentedly high levels of production and productivity. At the same time, however, by alienating the underprivileged majority from its role in the productive system it had sown the discontent which must provoke the revolution of the proletariat. According to the Marxian scenario, then, developments in technology and economic organization interacted with the associated changes in the structure of social relations to determine the quality as well as the pace of economic growth. However, the chief dynamic element in Marx's model of 'the evolution of the economic formation of society . . . viewed as a process of natural history' was economic rather than social. For him, technological progress was the prime mover in a continuous process of economic development:

Darwin has interested us in the history of Nature's Technology, i.e. in the formation of the organs of plants and animals, which organs serve as the instruments of production for sustaining life. Does not the history of the productive organs of man, or organs that are the material basis of all social organization deserve equal attention? . . . Technology discloses man's mode of dealing with Nature, the process of production by which he sustains his life, and thereby also lays bare the mode of formation of social relations, and the mental conceptions that flow from them . . .[7]

In the contemporary relevance and the historical and international sweep of his vision of the economic problems facing modern industrializing economies, Marx had no equal in his own time. None of the leading English economists of the 1850s and 1860s had gone as far as he in identifying the dynamic characteristics of large-scale industry or in analysing the causes and consequences of continuous technological change. Still less were they ready to take account of the related social and political implications and prospects when developing theories or policy prescriptions. Most theorists (whether English or continental) dealt with the social aspects of economic behaviour by fixing them in the initial assumptions of their theories, bottling them up into *ceteris paribus* clauses when stating economic laws, and relegating any unavoidable direct reference to them to situation-specific cases in applied economics. The notion that it was possible to distinguish between a science and an art of political economy was already embodied in the conventional wisdom of the discipline and acted as an excuse for excessively abstract economic theorizing which could masquerade as science. Meanwhile, the classical economists were too deeply committed to the view that the route to scientific truth in the social sciences led via a study of the rational behaviour of *individuals* to appreciate Marx's analysis of the class struggle. The prevailing consensus on methodological individualism was stated with confident clarity by John Stuart Mill, for example, in his *Logic*:

The laws of the phenomena of society are, and can be, nothing but the laws of the actions and passions of human beings united together in the social state. Men, however, in a state of society are still men; their actions and passions are obedient to the laws of human nature . . . Human beings in society have no properties but those which are derived from, and may be resolved into, the laws of the nature of the individual man.

Apart altogether, then, from the fact that Marx's system of economic theory was revolutionary rather than reformist in its apologetics, it is not surprising that his reconstruction of Ricardian economics should have made so little impact on mainstream economic thought during the nineteenth century. For, by treating the social aspects of economic change as endogenous to his model of long-term economic development, and by focusing on the behaviour of human beings as members of articulated social groups rather than as atomistic individuals, Marx in effect developed a system of theory that was too incompatible in scope and method with orthodox economic analysis to permit the reconciliation of differences through rational debate. The first volume of *Capital* (in German) appeared in 1867, when English classical economists were still basking in the high scientific repute currently attributed to them by public opinion. In 1861, for example, Sir James Stephen (not himself an economist) roundly asserted: 'That some departments of human conduct are capable of being classified with sufficient exactness to supply the materials of a true science is conclusively proved by the existence of Political Economy. Political Economists can appeal to the only test which really measures the truth of science—success— with as much confidence as astronomers.'

Such extravagant claims for a social science were doomed to disappointment. When the high noon of the mid-Victorian boom passed and entrepreneurial profits were squeezed between falling world prices and rising wage costs, Britain's commercial competitors began to return to protectionist policies, unemployment started to rise, and classical political economists found themselves again under attack for irrelevant and excessively abstract theorizing. Deepening depression in the 1870s showed up their inability to prescribe for continuous economic growth, threw doubt on their case for free trade, and underlined their failure to confront questions relating to the inequitable distribution of incomes. J.E. Cairnes, the leading British classical economist after Mill died, began his *Character and Logical Method of Political Economy* (1875) with a discussion of 'the present vacillating and unsatisfactory condition of the science in respect of fundamental principles'. The centenary of Adam Smith's *Wealth of Nations* provoked a flurry of laments for economics in

1876. Bonamy Price, then Professor of Political Economy at Oxford, took the occasion of his 1878 presidential address to the National Association for the Promotion of Social Science to explain some of the discredit into which the discipline had fallen by 'the grave mistake made by economists in attempting to give a scientific form to its teachings'. The Cambridge Professor of Political Economy, Henry Fawcett, continued to defend the orthodox doctrine surveyed in Mill's *Principles*, but was insufficiently interested in theoretical or philosophical issues to respond to the methodological critique then being mounted by the historical school.

The fact is that by the 1870s and 1880s, orthodox classical doctrine had already been overtaken by events—economic, social, and political. Its conceptual and theoretical framework was more relevant to a pre-industrial than to an industrial economy. The corn model at the heart of Ricardo's theory of economic growth, for example, was becoming an anachronism before Mill wrote his *Principles*, and the latter's obsession with Malthusian population arguments led to inplausible conclusions in a world of continuous technological progress. There was something increasingly far-fetched, moreover, about the classical emphasis on the consequences of diminishing (rather than increasing) returns, or on circulating (rather than fixed) capital, when large-scale highly capitalized industry was evidently becoming a dominant feature of the economic landscape.

Meanwhile, equally significant changes were taking place in the social and political context of economic behaviour. In Britain, for example, relations between capital and labour were being reshaped by the emergence of socially respectable trade unions on the one hand and by the Factory Acts on the other. The trend towards political democracy, which began hesitantly with the Reform Act of 1832, accelerated with the Acts of 1867 and 1884. The Act of 1867 extended the vote to the middle classes and to the urban working classes, that of 1884 took in the rural working men, while the Ballot Act of 1872, and a later Act to control corrupt practices, finally broke the power of the landed interests or the monied classes to rig parliamentary elections in their favour. Henceforth, the legislators whom it was the prime function of political economists to advise were forced by more than fine moral principles to take into account the interests of the working classes when framing their economic policies.

7

From political economy to economic science

> The nation used to be called the 'Body Politic'. So long as this phrase was in common use, men thought of the interests of the whole nation when they used the word 'Political' and then 'Political Economy' served well enough as a name for the science. But now 'political interests' generally mean the interests of only some part of parts of the nation; so that it seems best to drop the name 'Political Economy' and speak simply of *Economic Science*, or more shortly *Economics*.
>
> Alfred Marshall, 1879

Economists had been rubbing shoulders regularly with natural scientists at annual meetings of the British Association for the Advancement of Science since 1833, and—whatever their critics might say—most of them believed that they belonged in that league. The corollary was that they expected to advance their own discipline by adapting ideas, research techniques, and analytical methods that were evidently proving fruitful in the most successful hard sciences. Mid-century discussions of scientific method, stirred up by such well-known authorities as Comte's *Positive Philosophy* or Mill's *System of Logic*, tended to confirm these aspirations. However, when the consensus on fundamental principles (so essential to an established scientific discipline and so near the grasp of classical political economists in the 1820s and 1830s) began to slip away from them in the 1860s and 1870s, the way forward no longer seemed self-evident. It could no longer be taken for granted that it would ever be possible to discover and analyse regularities in social behaviour patterns by using abstract mechanical models similar to those which were effective in the physical sciences. At stake was the scientific status of political economy itself.

Broadly conceived, the role of the scientist is to describe and summarize reality in ways that might facilitate explanation, prediction, and control of a particular class of events. Given the complexity of the real world, his task necessitates a systematic process of selection, which is typically achieved by developing theories of the causal connections linking variables seen to be strategic in determining observable sequences of events. The more general the theory and the broader its vision, the more likely it is to elicit the commitment needed to stimulate a progressive research programme—particularly in the hard sciences where many of the phenomena under investigation tend to behave in essentially similar ways for successive generations of observers. The questions posed by natural scientists do of course change through time, as do their perceptions of their observational material when the accessible stock of testable empirical data widens and deepens. But for the most part, the real world they are examining changes slowly and predictably, if at all, and is little affected by their knowledge of it. It is different for social scientists. A theory designed to explain the behaviour of individuals or groups in an evolving social situation must be relatively specific as to time or place if it is to serve purposes of prediction or control. To the extent that decision-takers know what theory predicts for them, moreover, their behaviour tends to adapt in ways that make the theory either self-fulfilling or irrelevant. In any case, the more general the theory, the more abstract and remote it is likely to seem from the day-to-day concerns of practical policy-makers. It follows that a consensus among social scientists is both harder to complete and less durable. Indeed, a successful model of a rapidly-changing real world must be inherently flexible to remain true to its purpose.

The vision of economic reality, with its associated analytical frame-work and free trade policy prescriptions, which English classical economists had inherited from Smith and Ricardo had already begun to lose its charismatic quality in Britain when Mill set out to update it in his *Principles*. It had never been as fully accepted in Europe or North America. The fact that industrial progress in the 'workshop of the world' was evidently generating a widening incomes gap between rich and poor had already put the advocates of economic freedom on the defensive against their socialist critics. So when the international economic boom lost its impetus and turned into deepening depression in the 1870s, the need for a new vision—a politically more relevant perspective for economic theory and analysis—was widely felt by the acknowledged leaders of the discipline and not merely by its critics. In Germany and Austria, for example, where the numbers and prestige of academic economists had expanded in line with a vigorous expansion of the universities in the second half of the century, the debate on economic theory revolved around esoteric questions of methodology—the so-called *methodenstreit*—but actually reflected significant differences on the general objectives of economic enquiry. These differences were particularly sharp in relation to the role of the state in reconciling conflicts between economic interests, or maintaining economic justic, or promoting national economic growth or welfare. In Britain the debate was no less divisive in its socio-political implications and reflected similarly long-standing ideological tensions. But partly because the authoritative protagonists were fewer in number, their divisions were more readily papered over by a new orthodoxy which embodied enough of the old to be interpreted as the cumulative and progressive development of a solid corpus of economic knowledge.

The main force of the critique of English classical political economy came from two, diametrically opposed, directions. Walter Bagehot, one of the leading financial and political journalists of the Victorian era, pointed to the paradox in one of many articles published in celebration of the centenary of *The Wealth of Nations*: 'At the very moment that our Political Economy is objected to in some quarters as too abstract, in others an attempt is made to substitute for it one which is more abstract still. Mr Jevons of Manchester and M. Walras of Lausanne, without communication and almost simultaneously have worked out a 'mathematical' theory of Political Economy.' If the critics of orthodox economics were so diametrically opposed in their recommendations the classical economists might have been forgiven for inferring that their middle way must be the right track. But both sides in the attack were agreed with Jevons on one thing:

that Ricardo had 'shunted the car of Economic science on to a wrong line'. It was in any case hard to resist the conclusion that the Ricardian model was obsolete. The choice for would-be reformers seemed to lie between a 'realistic' historical school which tended to dissolve the boundaries between political economy and other social sciences, a mathematical school which theorized on the basis of exceedingly simple premises, and a 'neoclassical' solution which revised the existing corpus of economic theory in ways that made it more relevant to a modern political and economic context.

In the event, the reconstruction of economic theory which took place in the last three decades of the nineteenth century was shaped as much by recent trends in the general intellectual environment as by political or economic events. Not surprisingly, there were wide differences in the climate of ideas as between countries. In Britain, for example, recent advances in the life sciences on the one hand, and the gradual secularization of ethical doctrines on the other, assumed special significance for academics interested in the moral or social sciences. The Darwinian theory of evolution impinged heavily on their thinking for two reasons: first, because it matched their increasingly optimistic vision of the human development process; and secondly, because it clashed with the traditional anglicanism to which most university men were formally committed by their upbringing as well as, in the older universities such as Oxford and Cambridge, by the formal terms of their appointment.

For academics impressed by the potential of positive science, evolution by natural selection seemed virtually irrefutable. The essential breakthrough in biology had evidently emerged—long before Thomas Henry Huxley floored Bishop Wilberforce at the 1860 meeting of the British Association for the Advancement of Science—on the basis of imaginative scientific researches inspired and substantiated by many decades of careful accumulation and classification of zoological and botanical evidence, including the practical experience of animal or plant breeders who had identified and successfully fixed certain heritable characteristics of their subjects. Nor was it only eminent scientists and theologians who brought the argument about evolution into the public domain. Their popularizers enjoyed a much wider audience and succeeded in over-heating and polarizing educated opinion by injecting extremist speculations into reports of what was happening at the frontiers of scientific research.

The idea that development was an evolutionary process was not at all new in itself. Even the idea that men had evolved from monkeys was already part of the pseudo-scientific mythology of the eighteenth century. The French zoologist Lamarck (1744– 1829) was the first research scientist to publish an empirically based theory of evolution. That was in the early nineteenth century when he postulated an environmental mechanism of change; giraffes were supposed to grow long necks, for example, in response to changes in their ecological situation which encouraged them to browse in trees. True, Lamarck failed to convince his fellow-scientists or to impress his contemporaries and his theory did not gain wide circulation until Sir Charles Lyell presented it (in order to refute it) in his comprehensive *Principles of Geology* (1830–3). Thereafter, Lamarckian ideas frequently enlivened popular debates on human development. Robert Chambers, for example, founder of the famous Encyclopedia bearing his name, restated Lamarck's theory for popular consumption in his *Vestiges of the Natural History of Creation* (anonymously published in 1844), and Herbert Spencer, an even more influential popularizer of scientific theories (which he used as garnish for exciting cosmic speculations), adopted it several years later. Much later still, Lamarck's theory of evolution acquired a distinctive political connotation when it was invoked by Lysenko and Stalin in the course of twentieth-century debates on environment versus heredity as the chief agent of human development.

Although Lyell himself clung to the anti-evolutionary view that all living things originated in a divine act of creation, his three-volume treatise on geology—ambitiously subtitled 'an attempt to explain the former changes of the earth's surface by reference to causes now in operation'—gave the crucial encouragement to British scientists interested in evolution. This massive work of synthesis, ranging over palaeontology, ecology, and related aspects of biology, was the text which offered Charles Darwin an analytical framework for the observations he amassed during the five-year voyage of HMS *Beagle*—his first scientific project. More than a vade-mecum for diligent young scientists, Lyell's book became a natural history classic. In opening up new perspectives on the history of the earth and all its inanimate and animate content, Lyell succeeded in capturing the imagination not only of naturalists, but of all who believed in the essential unity of scientific knowledge. Here was a vision of open-ended geological time during which the earth's surface changed gradually in shape and content, accommodating in the process a continuous succession of living things which either adapted perfectly to ecological change or became extinct. The Cartesian vision of a clockwork universe (wound up by God at Genesis and set in predetermined motion until the Day of Judgement) became less compelling when, for the first time, natural history and human history were envisaged as a single continuous process of development. Lyell himself had been content with a traditional teleological explanation for the existing variety of living organisms, each species perfectly adapted to its ecological niche. In his own words, he accepted that 'it pleases the Author of Nature not simply to ordain fitness but the greatest fitness'. The new biologists, however, were not prepared to leave the matter there. Their problem was to discover the systematic laws of organic change, the dynamic mechanism by which species best fitted to survive adapted to shifts in their ecological context, while the least fitted were wiped out.

Significantly, each of the two biologists who arrived simultaneously and independently at the theory of evolution by natural selection in the 1850s—Charles Darwin and Alfred Russel Wallace —claimed to have been pointed in the right direction as a result of reading a treatise on political economy—Malthus's *Essay on the Principle of Population*. In Malthus's famous account of the 'struggle for life' inherent in populations with a geometrical growth potential and limited living space, they found the vital clue to their problem of formulating a biological law of evolution. For here was an explanation of how random genetic variations generated by large populations of individual species could eventually lead to the perpetuation of species characterized by superior ability to survive in a hostile or overcrowded environment.

There were some crucially debatable assumptions in the Darwinian solution to the problem—including, for example, the postulate of 'a strong principle of inheritance'. But the underlying assumption which fitted most comfortably with the ideological preconceptions characteristic of the mid-Victorian educated élite was that evolution by natural selection represented a continuous process of improvement in the conditions of life on earth. Darwin expressed this idea in the conclusion to his *Origin of Species* in almost polemical terms:

As all the living forms of life are the lineal descendants of those which lived long before the Silurian epoch, we may feel certain that the ordinary succession by generation has never been broken, and that no cataclysm has desolated the whole world. Hence we may look forward with some confidence to a secure future of equally inappreciable length. And as natural selection works solely by and for the good of each being, all corporeal and mental endowments will tend to progress towards perfection.

Economists brought up on the Smithian doctrine of the invisible hand—the belief that when every individual is free to maximize his own economic gain there will be a natural tendency for the economic gain of society as a whole to be maximized—would not find it hard to accept the last sentence of this passage.

In the circumstances of the mid-Victorian era, then, the message of Darwin's *Origin of Species* (1859) and *The Descent of Man* (1871) must have been particularly congenial to mainstream economists; and not simply because, as Darwin claimed: 'This is the doctrine of Malthus applied to the whole animal and vegetable kingdom.' More important was the fact that the social and political problems of an urbanizing, democratizing nation were making them increasingly sensitive to contemporary attacks on their *laissez-faire* policy bias. It was thus heartening to be able to take from Darwin a 'scientific' justification for the assumption that systematic *natural* forces were at work to ensure the ultimate welfare of the highest form of life—mankind. Indeed, there are passages where Darwin himself seemed to fall into the economists' own language of profit and loss when describing his theory, for example: 'Natural selection acts only by the preservation and accumulation of small inherited modifications, each profitable to the preserved being . . . Rejecting those that are bad, preserving and adding up all that are good, silently and insensibly working, whenever and wherever opportunity offers at the improvement of each organic being.' He also displayed a gratifying propensity for the kind of hypothetico-deductive reasoning which leading contemporary economists regarded as the best practice for their own discipline. It was not surprising, therefore, that the young Henry Fawcett, a devoted disciple of Mill and the future Cambridge Professor of Political Economy, became an enthusiastic convert to the Darwinian–Huxley line at the famous British Association confrontation between Huxley and Bishop Wilberforce in 1860. He went on to publish 'A Popular Exposition of Darwin's *Origin of Species*' in the December 1860 *Macmillan's Magazine* (which attracted Darwin's approval) and claimed proudly at the 1861 British Association meeting that 'Mr Darwin had strictly followed rules of the deductive method as laid down by John Stuart Mill.'

The popularizers of evolution theory went still further in providing psuedo-scientific credentials for orthodox economic doctrine. Herbert Spencer, for example, coined the phrase 'the survival of the fittest' to dramatize Darwin's theory and this soon entered the vocabulary of economists wishing to demonstrate the virtues of a freely competitive market and to justify objectively their bias towards *laissez-faire* policy prescriptions. Economists hankering after a scientific image for their discipline need not, it seemed, feel ashamed of their liberal economic assumptions. Plainly the Oxford Professor of Political Economy, Bonamy Price, who in 1878 lamented 'the grave mistake made by economists in attempting to give a scientific form to its teaching', was out of touch with current thinking at home and abroad. For it could be (and was) argued that political economy was not yet scientific enough.

The way forward was to develop a *purer* economic science, independently of its political and ethical implications, which could only confuse fundamental theoretical issues and make it unnecessarily hard to achieve the consensus essential to a cumulative advance of economic knowledge. Against this background of ideas, and with a shared conviction that there was urgent need for a new approach to economic theorizing, an English, an Austrian, and a French economist published, independently of each other and almost simultaneously, the three economic classics which are often credited with having launched the so-called marginal revolution in economics: W. S. Jevons, *Theory of Political Economy* (London, 1871); Karl Menger, *Grundsätze der Volkwirtschaftslehre* (Vienna, 1871); and Leon Walras, *Éléments d'économie politique* (Lausanne, 1874–7).

There were of course marked differences in the economic traditions within which British, Austrian, and French economists were reared in the mid nineteenth century, as well as in the nature of the contributions that Jevons, Menger, and Walras made to the future development of their discipline—nationally and internationally. To what extent these three authors jointly precipitated a *revolution* in the method and substance of economic analysis is debatable. What links them indissolubly in the history of economics is that each was convinced that it was necessary to reconstruct economic theory on more precise and abstract (hence more 'scientific') lines, that each focused on the theory of value as the Achilles' heel in the system of economic thought he wanted to revise, and that they were all dissatisfied with the Ricardian simplification which made value (or long-term price) depend primarily on cost of production to the virtual exclusion of demand factors. Associated with their focus on the theory of value (now reinterpreted as a theory of market exchange), and a new emphasis on the demand elements in the price equation, was a shared propensity to treat micro-economic theory as fundamental to all economic reasoning. This involved a retreat from the macro-economic questions and a narrowing of the scope of economic theory. In the longer run it meant downgrading applied economics as an academic pursuit; with the increasing professionalization of the discipline the best students were encouraged to concentrate their research efforts on abstract and theoretical, rather than practical and empirical, problems. Although none of the nineteenth-century leaders of the marginal revolution would have approved these tendencies, they were inherent in the distinction—already deeply embedded in the conventional wisdom of the discipline—between the positive science of economics and the art of political economy.

The virtually simultaneous appearance, in three geographically separate locations, of three substantive attempts to reconstruct the theoretical foundations of political economy on scientific lines, was largely coincidental. Evidence of an international consensus did, however, give an aura of authority to their shared preconceptions concerning the deficiencies of classical economics and to the common characteristics of their remedies. Much later (and with a strong dose of mid-twentieth-century hindsight) the episode was interpreted in histories of economic thought as the opening shots in an intellectual revolution—though it was actually quite early in the twentieth century that J. A. Hobson critically identified the concept of 'marginalism' as a dubious mechanical technique which was already distorting the perspective of British neo-classical analysis. Indeed it is arguable that only in Britain, where the Ricardo-Mill school had acquired what Jevons called the 'noxious authority' of a dogma, was a revolution in ideas needed to shatter orthodox doctrine, 'to fling aside once and for ever the mazy and presposterous assumptions of the Ricardian school', and start afresh. 'I protest', declaimed Jevons passionately in the concluding remarks to his *Theory of Political Economy*, 'against deference for any man, whether John Stuart Mill, or Adam Smith, or Aristotle, being allowed to check inquiry. Our science has become too much a stagnant one, in which opinions rather than experience and reason are appealed to.'

It was W. S. Jevons (1835–82), the British member of the famous trio, who could claim to have fired the first shot in the revolution with which they are now jointly credited. As a young man of 27 he had offered a sketch of his 'General Mathematical Theory of Political Economy' to the 1862 meeting of the British Association. But the time was not yet ripe for a brash newcomer to cloud the image of what was generally perceived as the most advanced of the social sciences, for—as he confided sadly to his journal—his paper was 'received without a word of interest or belief'. Even when it was printed in the 1866 *Journal of the Statistical Society* (of which Jevons was then a Fellow) it attracted little attention, although its author, the newly elected Cobden Professor of Political Economy at Manchester, had established his professional reputation with several imaginative contributions to economic statistics, including a widely read book on *The Coal Question* (1865) which predicted the imminent exhaustion of British coal reserves. By 1871, however, when Jevons published his *Theory of Political Economy*, he was not the only British academic translating economic theory into explicitly mathematical language. So although his first edition was unsympathetically reviewed by readers who were unwilling, or unable, to grapple with unfamiliar mathematics, and loftily criticized by the few who were already playing the same game (for example the young Alfred Marshall), this was the book that established Jevons's reputation for posterity. According to J. M. Keynes, for example, writing sixty-five years later for a centenary assessment of Jevons's life and work published in the 1936 *Journal of the Royal Statistical Society*: 'Jevons' *Theory* is the first treatise to present in a finished form the theory of value based on subjective valuations, the marginal principle and the now familiar technique of the algebra and diagrams of the subject. The first modern book on economics, it has proved singularly attractive to bright minds newly attacking the subject: simple, lucid, unfaltering, chiselled in stone where Marshall knits in wool.'[1]

Nevertheless, it was not Jevons but Marshall who was to found the new orthodoxy that took shape in the United Kingdom in the last three decades of the century. Jevons himself died too young—the victim of a drowning accident at the age of 46—before the distinctive quality of his theorizing was understood, still less appreciated, by most of his British contemporaries. He had barely had time to plan the more comprehensive 'Principles of Economics' that he intended as his chief magnum opus. By 1871 his *Theory of Political Economy* had attracted sufficient attention to go into a second edition, but it remained too far out of line with contemporary trends in economic thinking to have a powerful direct impact on leading economists. His stress on subjective utility as the prime determinant of market value was overstated— for instance in insisting that 'Value depends *solely* on the final degree of utility'—while his chapter on the 'noxious influence of authority' was more abrasive than persuasive. At the same time, his strong endorsement of the Benthamite felicific calculus seemed quaint to an intellectual community under the influence of Mill's and Sidgwick's more diluted utilitarianism. Indeed the commonest accusation made against Jevons was that he was a hedonist, a charge that labelled his economic philosophy as too old-fashioned to be taken seriously by modern thinkers.

It is now evident that he was ahead of his time in certain crucial respects: for example, when Jevons (1) focused on the theory of exchange as the core of a positive science of economics; (2) used the concept of marginal utility as a master key to the theory of value; and (3) recognized that the only practical problem which a mathematically rigorous theory was capable of handling objectively was the static problem of allocating given resources to produce an optimum return, he was pointing precisely in the direction eventually taken by orthodox neoclassical economics. This, however is a judgement of hindsight. In the 1870s, the intellectual community of economists, uneasily divided by the failure of classical theory to measure up to the contemporary economic problem situation, was not at all receptive to the notion that the first step towards a genuinely scientific consensus was to construct a general mathematical theory of value. On the contrary, they were more shaken by charges of unscientific method currently being levelled at them from the opposite direction, that is, by historical economists who accused them of being too abstract and too unrealistic in their theories and analytical procedures.

So it was that during the period of little more than a decade between the first edition of Jevons's *Theory of Political Economy* and his premature death in 1882, the developing critique of orthodox economic theory was fired less by his campaign for a mathematical approach than by the wholly plausible complaint that it lacked a sound empirical base. Contemporary methodological debates revolved around the tension between inductive and deductive techniques of acquiring reliable knowledge. For the historicists claimed confidently that theirs was the true scientific methodology. The view that the standard method of the natural sciences was to begin by building up a solid basis of factual observations in order to derive general laws from agreed facts was already a familiar stereotype in the nineteenth century. Most leading natural scientists paid it lip service, though they were often ambivalent towards it in practice. For example, Charles Darwin wrote in his autobiography that when he started out on his biological researches he 'worked on true Baconian principles and without any theory collected facts on a wholesale scale'. But in a letter written to young Henry Fawcett in 1861, he put forward a significantly different view of scientific method: 'About 30 years ago there was much talk that geologists ought only to observe and theorize; and I well remember someone saying that at this rate a man might as well go into a gravel-pit and count the pebbles and describe the colours. How odd it is that anyone should not see that all observations must be for or against some view if it is to be of any service.'

The historical school of political economy originated in Germany, where it represented an empiricist reaction against English classical political economy (particularly the extremely deductive Ricardian style of analysis) and drew inspiration from recent developments in biological science. Gustav von Schmoller, a representative of the second generation of German historical economists, was to announce in his inaugural address to the Prussian Academy of Sciences in 1887 his ambition to 'completely free the science from the dogma of the Anglo-French utilitarian philosophy and to base it on another more profound and secure psychological and historical edifice'.

When confidence in the classical orthodoxy wilted in the 1870s in England it was two Irish academics who took the lead in publicizing the German alternative. They were J. K. Ingram (1823–1907) and T. E. Cliffe Leslie (1826–82). Of the two, Cliffe Leslie was the better economist. He had published a scholarly research work on comparative land systems (under the influence of the legal historian Sir Henry Maine) and he was the more incisive critic of orthodox economic theory. However, Ingram, a historian with limited analytical skill, reached the wider audience. He had made an impression on the intellectual community with his resounding address at the 1878 British Association meeting, where he pontificated on 'The Present Position and Prospects of Political Economy' and confidently announced the birth of a 'new economics'. More widely circulated, however, was his *History of Political Economy* (originally commissioned for the 1885 *Encyclopedia Britannica*), which went through several English editions in book form, including German and Russian translations.

It was not a distinguished history of economic thought, but it was the first of its kind and it summarized a historical school specification for the economic science of the future. There were four features of the new approach as formulated by Ingram: (1) The new economics would take its place as a sub-discipline of the 'one great Science of Sociology', merely 'a separate chapter which must be kept in close relation to the others'; (2) 'Economic Science like Sociology in general must be—to employ the useful terminology of Comte—not statical but also dynamical' and would therefore start from the assumption that 'no social fact can be understood apart from its history'; (3) It would abandon the concept of Economic Man and follow the lead of the other positive sciences by first ascertaining 'what the social facts are and only after this inquiry has been completed endeavour to trace them to their sources in the constitution of the external world, in human nature and in the contemporary circumstances of Society'; (4) Finally, the new economics would display 'new tendencies in sentiment and moral tone', thus banishing the spectre of the 'dismal science' and attracting the best minds of future generations to its study.

All this was rhetoric rather than reasoned argument and was not intrinsically persuasive. However, university economists, who were to become the leading representatives of an emergent economics profession in the later decades of the nineteenth century, were driven to take the historical economists more seriously than they might otherwise have done for two reasons. The first was their vulnerability to the charge that laws of political economy lacked scientific validity unless adequately supported by empirical data. The second was that the academic prestige of history itself had risen rapidly during the nineteenth century. When the historians also succumbed to the cult of science, history ceased to be primarily a vehicle for literary brilliance or romantic polemics and began to infiltrate surprisingly influential Trojan horses into the camps of the more austere social sciences. John Seeley (the first Regius Professor of Modern History at Cambridge) announced the new role for history as early as 1863: 'It is the special work of the present age to give a historical basis, in other words a basis of fact, to moral science. And therefore in the present age *history* considered as the possible basis of a science begins to wear a new aspect and to assume a new importance.'

These imperialist designs were given impetus by an impressive series of research monographs documenting the history of human progress on the basis of a most meticulous, often exhaustive, sometimes critical, exploitation of primary sources. There was, for example, Henry Maine's *Ancient Law* (1861), which revealed the potential of the 'comparative method' of history; there was William Stubbs's two volumes of *Rolls Series*, his volume of *Select Charters*, and, most influential of all, his monumental *Constitutional History of England* (1874–8), which told the success story of the English parliamentary system. Additionally there were painstaking compilations of data on economic history—such as Thorold Rogers' seven-volume *History of Agriculture and Prices in England* (1866–1902)—which supplied ammunition to political economists seeking a suitable selection of historical facts to support their arguments. Such immensely detailed chronicles seemed, in a Darwinian age, more like sound science than anything the classical economists had produced, not least because they provided evidence for the inexorable progress of civilization as defined by mid-Victorian liberals. It was thus not altogether surprising that history was recognized as an independent discipline at Cambridge as early as 1873, a generation before political economy achieved the status of an independent Tripos there. Significantly, and also a sign of the times, the economic historian Thorold Rogers was twice elected to the Drummond chair of political economy in Oxford (in 1866 and again in 1878), though his rather conventional brand of economic analysis was never allowed to invade his historical chronicles.

The economist who effectively reconstructed classical political economy and became the acknowledged leader of a new orthodoxy for English-speaking economists was Alfred Marshall (1852–1924). Renamed economics instead of political economy when Marshall's *Priciples of Economics* (1890) became its standard text, the new orthodoxy was more robust and more widely acceptable (even in continental circles) than the old, for what a German reviewer, Adolf Wagner, was to call its 'mediating attitude' restored disciplinary confidence to an intellectual community which had suffered half a century of doubt and dissension. More important still, because it opened up a variety of exciting and important new research horizons for professional economists, it proved remarkably durable. When Joseph Schumpeter (1883–1950), a product of the Austrian school of marginalists, addressed the 1927 British Association (to which he was invited as a distinguished visiting professor from the University of Bonn) he could be unequivocally concise on the question of economic method: 'It will shorten matters and facilitate exposition if I state at the outset that, barring differences on a number of particular points, the following results run entirely on Marshallian lines. But I could equally well call them Walrasian lines. For within serious economic theory there are no such things as 'schools' or differences of principle, and the only fundamental cleavage in modern economics is between good work and bad.' Undoubtedly he was exaggerating the degree of harmony prevailing in the international community of economists. But few contemporary theorists would have contradicted him, even if some applied economists would have been highly sceptical. What was certain was that by the 1920s *methodenstreit* had ceased to agitate the academic debates and that for university teachers of economics the level of professional consensus on economic theory was comfortably high—higher than it had ever been before, or indeed since for a comparable length of time.

When Alfred Marshall went up to Cambridge to read for the Mathematical Tripos in the early 1860s it was in the earnest expectation of taking holy orders and with the hope of ranking highly enough in his final examinations to be admitted to a college fellowship which would guarantee him an academic career. His fellowship was soon won, for he was a keen mathematician and ranked second among the 1865 Wranglers (first-class honours graduates in the Mathematics Tripos). But ordination no longer figured in his plans. For the intellectual conflict between science and religion stirred up by the Darwinian controversies reached a climax in the mid-1860s; and university men who cared deeply about both were obliged to re-examine their religious beliefs. Few of them were sufficiently decisive in choosing between reason and dogma to follow the dramatic example of Henry Sidgwick, who resigned his Trinity fellowship in 1869 because he could no longer subscribe fully to the Thirty-nine Articles to which all Oxford and Cambridge fellows were obliged to swear adherence on first appointment. Trinity College, however, reflected the spirit of the age when it responded to Sidgwick's resignation by appointing him instead to the unestablished post of lecturer in moral sciences. Two years later, in 1871, the Bill to abolish religious tests in Oxford and Cambridge (which had been annually put before Parliament from 1863) finally passed into the Act allowing the dons who had (like Sidgwick) 'taken service with reason' to pursue the quest for scientific truth without wrestling endlessly with their consciences.

To the new don teaching mathematics at St John's College, Alfred Marshall, the impact of the science versus religion debates was dominated by the powerful moral influence of Henry Sidgwick (he was to refer to him much later as 'my spiritual mother and father') and had the effect of diverting him from higher mathematics and molecular physics towards the relatively messy and unprestigious moral sciences. An autobiographical fragment written in 1917, and intended as a preface to his *Money Credit and Commerce* (1922), described his own intellectual journey through metaphysics and psychology, the last of which 'brought me in touch with the question: how far do the conditions of life of the British (and other) working classes generally suffice for the fullness of life? Older and wiser men told me that the resources of production do not suffice for affording to the great body of people the leisure and opportunity for study; and they told me that I needed to study Political Economy. I followed their advice, and regarded myself as a wanderer in the land of dry facts; looking forward to a speedy return to the luxuriance of pure thought.'[2]

So it was that in 1867 Marshall, after working his way through Mill's *Principles* began to amuse himself by translating Ricardian and Smithian theories into mathematics. In 1868 he was appointed special lecturer in moral sciences at St John's and began teaching economics to undergraduates, though it was not until the early 1870s that—finding political economy the most academically neglected of the moral sciences—he made it the principal focus of his own research effort.

When Marshall succeeded Fawcett to the Cambridge chair of political economy in 1885 he had published only one book—a popular textbook written in collaboration with his wife (an ex-pupil) and designed for Cambridge extra-mural courses. But he was already the acknowledged leader of what contemporaries were calling the 'new school of political economy'. H.S. Foxwell, for example, when commissioned to write an article on current economic thinking in England for the October 1887 issue of the American *Quarterly Journal of Economics*, cast Marshall as the moving spirit in a new theoretical approach flowing from the convergence of three lines of constructive criticism—the idealist, the mathematical, and the historical. Of Marshall himself, Foxwell asserted that: 'Half the economic chairs in the United Kingdom are occupied by his pupils and the share taken by them in general economic instruction in England is even larger than this.' He was not exaggerating.

Before the first edition of Marshall's *Principles of Economics* (1890) went to press the majority of the admittedly small band of university teachers of economics had been acquainted with its main thrust and style of analysis—at second hand if not by the master himself. It was reviewed with considerable respect nationally and internationally, even by its critics. William Ashley, for example, the historical economist who wrote for the *Economic Journal* in 1891 a devastating critique of the 'rehabilitation of Ricardo' which Marshall had smuggled into his *Principles*, nevertheless described him as the 'doyen of English economists', and went on to acclaim the new text in the following terms: 'It casts into the background almost all that has been written in England since John Stuart Mill; it sums up the economic movement of the last forty years, and furnishes the point of departure for a new and fruitful development. It is the more welcome because it brings a message of conciliation to divergent schools and makes it possible for "deductive" and "historical", "scientific" and "ethical" economists to work together in harmony. But it has the defects of its qualities . . .' and as Ashley had amply demonstrated, Marshall's interpretation of Ricardo's message was more 'sympathetic' than historically defensible.

The fact is that Marshall was determined not to be seen as a revolutionary in economic theory. On the contrary he was obsessively concerned to pursue an evolutionary approach when analysing progress in economic science—as well as in political and economic development generally. The motto on the title page of his *Principles* reads 'Natura non facit saltum'—which was also Darwin's touchstone—and the preface to the first edition spelt out the motif at length. After announcing that his book was no more than 'an attempt to present a modern version of old doctrines with the aid of new work and with reference to the problems of our age', Marshall insisted that in so far as it had 'any special character of its own' it lay in applying the 'Principle of Continuity' as a fundamental idea in a reconstructed economic theory.

The idea of continuity was of course central to the Jevonian and Walrasian mathematical techniques of analysis, and Marshall brought it into play with a reference to 'the fact that our observations of nature, in the moral as in the physical world, related not so much to aggregate quantities as to increments of quantities, and that in particular the demand for a thing is a continuous function, of which the 'marginal' increment is, in stable equilibrium, balanced against the corresponding increment of its cost of production. It is not easy to get a full clear view of continuity in this aspect without the aid either of mathematical symbols or of diagrams.' Unlike Jevons, however, Marshall (1) relegated the mathematical symbols and diagrams to footnotes and appendices (on the grounds that they had illustrative and clarificatory value only), and (2) gave marginal productivity an interdependent role with marginal utility as joint determinants of equilibrium value. 'We might as reasonably dispute', he said characteristically in the *Principles*, 'whether it is the upper or the underblade of a pair of scissors which cuts a piece of paper as whether value is governed by utility or cost of production.' Again the preface invoked the biological analogy: 'As, in spite of the great differences between birds and quadrupeds, there is one Fundamental Idea running through all their frames, so the general theory of the equilibrium of demand and supply is a Fundamental Idea running through all the various parts of the central problem of Distribution and Exchange.'

Later generations of economists would find Marshall's biological analogies far-fetched, but to contemporaries they had a convincingly modern ring. They embellished a general approach designed to reach a wider educated public than either the mathematical economists (such as Jevons or Walras) or the militant historicists (such as William Cunningham) were able to interest. Economists who had acquired their economic theory from the classic texts could relate confidently to a new version which (a) embodied many of the salient features of the old; (b) did not centrally involve unfamiliar mathematical arguments; (c) introduced a well-integrated package of new analytical concepts and techniques readily applicable in a variety of contexts; and (d) was presented as part of a scientifically progressive research programme rather than as a new economic gospel.

This last characteristic of the Marshallian approach was the most novel and durable consequence of his commitment to the idea of evolution. The passage in his inaugural lecture at Cambridge with which he extricated political economy from the false position of being a repository of simple economic truths and infallible policy prescriptions still has inspirational force for economists in the late twentieth century: '. . . that part of economic doctrine which alone can claim universality has no dogmas. It is not a body of concrete truth but an engine for the discovery of concrete truth.'[3] A decade later, buoyed up by the success of his *Principles* as a teaching instrument, Marshall developed this theme in another speech to Cambridge students, published in the 1897 *Economic Journal*. There he contrasted a new generation of economists, trained to reason their way to a solution of modern economic problems by applying the resources of an efficient analytical tool-box, with a past generation operating from a set of general principles which had been misleadingly 'bold and peremptory':

Never again will a Mrs Trimmer, or a Mrs Marcet, or a Miss Martineau earn a goodly reputation by throwing them into a form of a catechism or of simple tales, by aid of which any intelligent governess might make clear to the children nestling around her where lies economic truth, and might send them forth to instruct statesmen and merchants how to choose the right path in economic policy, and to avoid the wrong. It is now patent, even to those who are in a hurry, that no practical economic problems can be settled offhand by appeal to general doctrines; for the things of which account must be taken are so diverse, and our knowledge of them so slight, that they yield no firm hold for formal proof. Much must be taken on conjecture; much must be decided by commonsense rather than by reasoning on strictly logical lines. Thus the growing perfection of scientific machinery in economics, so far from lessening the responsibilities of commonsense, increases those responsibilities.[4]

In short, the day of the journalistic amateur political economist was over. The future lay with a research-minded community of economic scientists who were capable of marrying imagination with technical expertise.

Evidently, however, the economic scientist was not expected to retreat to an academic ivory tower. The new generation of economists was as fully dedicated as their predecessors to solving urgent practical policy problems, though Marshall never claimed that the theories developed in his *Principles* were more than a first step on the way to acquiring reliable economic knowledge. Nevertheless, he expected the cumulative results of systematic economic research to be useful and accessible to practical men of business as well as to legislators, and his implicit specification for the competent economist included an insatiable hunger for facts, high moral principles, and a trained commonsense, as well as an ability to manipulate the 'scientific machinery' of pure theory. Nor did Marshall find it necessary to hide his ideological preconceptions. Indeed the fact that these were shared by most members of the late-Victorian middle class and were essentially similiar to those of the classical economists made it easier to present the new economic orthodoxy as a lineal descendant of the old.

In particular, for example, Marshall was strongly anti-socialist and individualist in his approach to policy issues. His faith in the potential of free competitive industry to raise the material and immaterial quality of human living standards generally was absolute. He was of course aware that the march of economic and political events—the expansion of large-scale industry, for example, or the extension of the vote and of educational opportunities to the working classes—made it necessary to re-examine the role of the state and to detach economics from doctrinaire opinions on *laissez-faire*.

In his presidential address in 1890 to the Economics Section of the British Association Marshall frankly exposed the crucial elements in his new packaging for the old ideology. Protection, for example, was admitted to have some temporary advantages for underdeveloped economies, but for countries such as Britain and America the free trade arguments remained irrefutable. Trade unions deserved encouragement, partly because class justice demanded that the workers be given a stronger leverage in the wage bargain, but more because free collective bargaining would help employees 'to get a substantial though not a great increase of real wages: which they may, if they will, so use as to increase their efficiency, and therefore to increase still further the wages which they are capable of earning, whether acting in combination or not'. The need for a measure of public control, even possibly ownership, of public utilities which operated more efficiently on monopolistic lines could not be denied. But Marshall revolted against the very idea of direct intervention by the political authorities and advocated management by public corporations— for reasons that were far from scientific or objective: 'We (for I would here include myself) believe that bureaucratic management is less suitable for Anglo-Saxon than for other races who are more patient and more easily contented, more submissive and less full of initiative, who like to take things easily and to spread their work over long hours.'

Given his Darwinian faith in a naturally beneficent process of evolution on the one hand, and his classical (Smithian) mistrust of political intervention in the free market on the other, it is not surprising that Marshall should have been inclined to minimize the role of the State as an agent of economic development. What was more significant for the history of ideas, however, was that in focusing his main theoretical research effort on micro-economic questions he effectively ignored the sort of macro-economic issues in which central government policy must be the prime mover. The new generation of economists brought up on Marshall's *Principles* were similarly blinkered. However, they were endowed with two positive advantages over their predecessors: they were fired by the conviction that they were in at the start of an infinitely progressive research programme; and they were equipped with special 'scientific machinery'—an analytical apparatus which could also evolve to greater perfection in the hands of the intelligent and enthusiastic user. One of the new generation, D. H. Macgregor, who had taken Marshall's lectures in the early years of the twentieth century, was to look back in 1942 at the start of a new age for professional economists:

In my time there was no other book you had to know about but the *Principles*. We did not read Adam Smith. We knew hardly anything at all about Marx. The historical school was liable to dangerous fallacy. There was a bedrock, which was the truth, and the way to get it was by the use of analysis. We were soaked and stewed in the theory of Value. The intelligentsia of undergraduates who now, building from the roof down mutter 'liquidity preference' as their key idea, then sweated in puzzled faith over consumers' surplus, short-period value and quasi-rent.

8

Economic science in an
unstable world economy

Perhaps the chief task of economists at this hour is to
distinguish afresh the *Agenda* of government from the
Non-Agenda; and the companion task of politics is to
devise forms of government within a democracy which
shall be capable of accomplishing the *Agenda*.

J.M. Keynes (1926)

By the early twentieth century the new economics was offering a
distinctive intellectual challenge to university students concerned
by the policy problems of a modern industrial society. They could
now embark on a specialized programme of reading to equip
themselves with the basic information, theoretical framework,
and analytical techniques relevant to a purportedly objective
social science. Its textbooks described a broad international consensus on the theories and concepts needed to analyse patterns of
behaviour in a competitive market economy. Their central uni-
fying theme was a new theory of value—essentially a theory of
the way market prices were determined in conditions of competitive equilibrium—which assumed away some of the philosophical
tensions and ambiguities inherent in classical political economy;
and they deployed an integrated set of simple mathematical tools
and concepts over a wide range of realistic and important economic questions.

Students aspiring to apply their analytical equipment to problems arising in business decision-making, or public policy formulation, or academic research, were encouraged (sometimes
elated) by the intellectual self-confidence exuded by the heirs of
what was rapidly becoming the neo-classical orthodoxy. J.M.
Keynes, for example, who celebrated his first-class honours
degree in the Cambridge Mathematical Tripos by reading 'masses

of economics' in the summer of 1905, was stimulated to write in November to his friend Lytton Strachey: 'I find Economics increasingly satisfactory and I think I am rather good at it. I want to manage a railway or organise a Trust or at least swindle the investing public. It is so easy and fascinating to understand the principle of these things.'

Now that the arid disputes on fundamental principles had receded into history, the controversies which enlivened this politically oriented discipline could revolve fruitfully around the urgent policy questions calling for systematic research. Ambitious young economists were stimulated by the undogmatic, forward-looking stance of the acknowledged leaders of their discipline (such as Alfred Marshall) to believe that they themselves could make worthwhile contributions to the advancement of economic knowledge. Dennis Robertson, for example, who began to read economics in 1910, reflected later on the buoyant spirit in which his generation took up the challenge:

We thought we knew pretty well what sort of things we wanted to know about and were glad to take the counsel given by Marshall himself near the beginning of the *Principles*: 'the less we concern ourselves with scholastic enquiries as to whether a certain consideration comes within the scope of economics the better.'

Moreover, in spite of a propensity on the part of the academic élite to identify the scientific content of economics with pure theory, what the new generation of economists focused on was dictated to a large extent by the substance of current policy issues. Problems of tariff policy, unemployment, industrial fluctuations, and international monetary organization, for example, stood high on the research agenda of British economists on the eve of the First World War.

The stage thus seemed to be set for a cumulative advancement of positive economic knowledge in an area which educated public opinion judged to be of immediate importance. However, the possibility of finding useful answers to current policy questions within the framework of the new economic orthodoxy depended on the relevance to actual conditions and events of its key assumptions and analytical techniques; and that in turn depended not only on the realism of the new world-view embodied in the new economic science, but also on the stability of the economic system it was designed to interpret.

In the event, the First World War crucially destabilized many of the economic trends and patterns of behaviour on which late nineteenth-century economists had based their theories. In particular, for example, it injected far-reaching command elements into the markets for goods and services and money, it accelerated structural changes which had been barely perceptible before the turn of the century, and it transformed the expectations and objectives of decision-takers in both private and public sectors. The fact that most of these shifts were perceived—by analogy with the special upheavals of war and its aftermath—as temporary disturbances in a generally stable politico-economic environment did not make it easy for decision-takers to resume pre-war behaviour patterns. On the contrary, those who hankered in the 1920s after the relative stability of the pre-1914 era were chasing a mirage. For the destructive effects of a global war, together with the political and economic turmoils of its international aftermath, had had profound implications for the anatomy and operation of the world economy. In these circumstances, obstinate ambitions to 'put the clock back' tended to distract attention from the new long-term problems for which policy-makers urgently required answers.

The outstanding characteristic of the world economy in the six or seven decades before 1914—certainly the characteristic which distinguished it most sharply from that of the inter-war period—had been a high and growing degree of market integration. The spread of modern manufacturing industry from the original industrial core countries (Britain, France, Belgium, Germany, and the United States) to nations such as Russia, Japan, Italy, Canada, and the Scandinavian countries, plus the extension of their direct trade with the primary producing regions in the rest of the world, was associated with a revolution in international communications which brought North and South America, Australia, and Asia into a single market with Europe. Never in the history of the world had there been such a free movement of goods, factors of production, and technological knowledge between nations and continents. It offered substantial rewards to those with the initiative, resources, and skills to respond to economic opportunity. The developing regions of the New World enjoyed access to flexible supplies of manpower and finance needed to exploit a rich reservoir of natural resources, while their development booms gave the mature industrial nations of the Old World a safety valve to relieve cyclical problems of unemployment or over-investment.

The First World War checked the bonanza and reversed the tendencies towards global integration. Four years of intensive concentration on the war effort by the main belligerents distorted the peacetime channels of trade, diverted exports of capital from productive to destructive uses and restructured patterns of international comparative advantage. Some countries emerged from the First World War and its aftermath more productive than when they had entered it. In the United States, for example, manufacturing output was 22 per cent above its 1913 level by 1920 and 41 per cent above in 1923. In Europe, on the other hand, manufacturing output was 23 per cent below the 1913 level in 1920 and still 8 per cent below by 1923. The inevitable disruption of liberal economic relationships involved in the war itself was further intensified during its aftermath by a multiplication of national frontiers, a crippling load of war debts and reparations, and the spread of economic nationalism. In Soviet Russia, Fascist Italy, and from the 1930s Nazi Germany the State began directly to control and manipulate the national economy to serve political ends. Most of the industrial core countries faced unprecedented levels of industrial unemployment and excess capital capacity and responded by surrounding their domestic markets with a thicket of trade and currency barriers. Even in the United Kingdom, the traditional bastion of free trade, there was a retreat into the protection of strategic industries. In short, the expansion and integration which had boosted the world economy of the 1870–1914 era gave way to widespread stagnation and disintegration in the inter-war years.

Five interrelated aspects of the changed institutional environment had significant implications for the relevance of mainstream economic theory in the inter-war period and after. The first arose out of change in the international financial system and bore particularly on monetary theory. The second was the result of an essentially ideological shift—a pervasive change in the popular perceptions of the role of government in the national economy. The third was the decline in the level of competition associated with changes in the scale, structure, and organization of modern commerce and industry. The fourth was a change in the character of the labour market, resulting from such social trends as population growth and urbanization, the spread of literacy, the extension of the parliamentary franchise, and the maturation of trade unions. The fifth was a marked increase in the degree of political, economic, and financial uncertainty affecting day-to-day market decisions at both the micro- and macro-economic level.

It was in relation to monetary policy that the post-war problems proved most immediate and challenging. Curiously, the reconstruction of economic theory involved in the switch from classical political economy to neo-classical economic science had bypassed the theory of money. It is curious because monetary matters never ceased to stand high on the economists' agenda of applied research problems, and also because there were substantial evolutionary changes (as well as international variations) in the structure and role of financial institutions and monetary instruments over the half century preceding the First World War. It was not that leading theorists ignored monetary theory. Walras, for example, wove money into his theory of general equilibrium. Wicksell's posthumous international fame as an innovative monetary theorist outshone that of most of his contemporaries, though he had little influence in his own lifetime except in Sweden. Marshall had, according to Keynes, worked out a coherent theory of money as early as 1875. True, his long promised textbook on *Money, Credit and Commerce* did not reach the booksellers until 1923, though its message supported a fertile oral tradition as demonstrated by a stream of distinguished books and articles signed by his Cambridge disciples. Nevertheless, such progress as occurred in the theory of money in the early part of the twentieth century was consistent with a classical framework of analysis and built largely on foundations set out in

J. S. Mill's *Principles*. A. C. Pigou, in his 1939 presidential address to the Royal Economic Society, was to attribute his own generation's failure to innovate in this area to the overpowering dominance of Marshall. 'What was the use', he asked, 'of anyone working at Money, when we knew that in his head if not in his drawer there was an analysis enormously superior to anything we could hope to accomplish.' Not until the catastrophe of the First World War and its aftermath had destroyed the international financial system and ushered in an era of unbalanced budgets did it become urgent to reconstruct the traditional theory of money. Meanwhile, the convention of keeping the theory of money in a separate analytical compartment from the theory of value, and of treating the value of money itself as a neutral factor, no more than a veil which had negligible significance in relation to long-run trends of aggregate real output or income, continued to dominate mainstream neo-classical theory as completely as it had classical theorizing.

The international financial system based on gold fell apart when the leading belligerents responded to the outbreak of war by suspending convertibility in order to protect their gold reserves. Suspension was then regarded as a temporary measure and no one doubted that the nineteenth century gold standard would be restored as soon as the emergency was over. In retrospect, it is evident that the legendary stability of that system rested on two sacred pillars—consensus on Ricardian monetary theory on the one hand, and the dominant role of the United Kingdom as the global centre of international trade and payments on the other. For the United Kingdom itself the system can be dated from 1821 when the pound sterling was restored to the value it had held from 1717 until the 1797 Suspension of Cash Payments precipitated by the French wars. The formal rules of operation were subsequently embodied in the Bank Charter Act, which gave the Bank of England responsibility for *automatically* regulating the nation's money supply by contracting or expanding credit when gold flowed out of or into the country. The rationale behind this piece of legislation was the conviction (rooted in a simplistic quantity theory of money) that if the nation's money supply was thus regulated by an apolitical authority with a statutory duty to convert banknotes into gold at a fixed rate, the real value of the pound sterling would be held firm, explosive crises of confidence would be eliminated, and domestic price fluctuations contained.

The Bank Charter Act did not operate as smoothly as its authors had predicted. If anything, the rate of price change after 1844 was greater than it had been before. Nor did it eliminate financial panics. There were actually three crises (in 1847, 1857, and 1866) when the political authorities suspended the Act so as to permit the Bank to relax credit against the rules, thus checking the spread of domestic bankruptcies. Nevertheless, the currency of the dominant trading nation was firmly fixed in terms of gold for almost a century, 1821–1914; and as the nineteenth century wore on, all leading trading countries either went on to the gold standard, or attached themselves to it indirectly, by holding their monetary reserves in currencies fixed in terms of gold. By the turn of the century there existed a solid core of stable foreign exchange relationships based firmly on gold.

A variety of explanations have been advanced for the remarkable stability of the pre-1914 gold standard, many of them informed by hindsight. What is interesting about this episode in relation to the evolution of monetary theory, however, is that there was then a broad consensus concerning the operative reasons for the success of the system. It was a notable example of the way popular confidence in the validity of monetary theory contributes to the success of policies based on it. Although the rationale for the gold standard system assumed a naïve concept of money as equivalent to notes and coin, and although the eleven leading central banks involved in the pre-1914 gold standard did not always obey the implicit 'rules of the game' as strictly or as automatically as the formal system required, no one questioned its basic rationale. The underlying assumption was that the best guarantee of a sound monetary system was to attach it to a metallic standard —either gold or a combination of gold and silver. When the currencies of all the major trading nations were convertible into gold there was of course no need to raise awkward questions about what gold itself was worth, or whether it was wise to export capital to a gold standard country with a deficit on the balance of payments.

Not surprisingly, once the conventional discipline of the gold standard had been renounced in 1914, soaring war expenditures precipitated first a massive world-wide inflation and then a post-war restocking boom. In Britain over the six years 1914–20 there had been an average rate of price increase amounting to 18 per cent annum. In most of Europe the rate of inflation was higher and some European countries (including Germany, Russia, and Austria) stampeded into hyper-inflation on a scale which destroyed their currencies. The contrast with United Kingdom experience is instructive. There, faith in nineteenth-century canons of sound finance never wavered. Once the war was over and the victory objective no longer overrode all other aims, fiscal policy was again directed towards balancing the central government budget and steadily converting the swollen floating debt into long-term funded debt. Monetary policy also reverted sharply to pre-war canons. The post-war boom was checked by raising the Bank Rate to 7 per cent and by holding it there, in the teeth of falling prices, for more than a year. By then boom had turned into deep slump which lasted until early 1923.

At that stage, as far as the United Kingdom was concerned, recovery was smothered by the determination of the authorities not only to return to gold (an objective which was not itself a matter for serious contention) but to return at the pre-war parity for sterling. The trouble was that the restrictive monetary and fiscal policies needed to force up the foreign exchange value of a chronically weak pound discouraged domestic investment, aggravated the unemployment problem, and inhibited the structural readjustments required by British industries suffering from capital obsolescence and lagging competitiveness in world markets. As it turned out, the British return to gold did not help to stabilize the international financial system because the United Kingdom no longer dominated world trade and was itself swept off gold in the panic scramble for liquidity which followed the failure of a major Austrian investment bank in 1931. It had taken more than a decade for the British monetary authorities to come to grips with the fact that the pre-war system of economic relationships was beyond repair and that their attempts to put the clock back were doomed to be self-defeating.

The events of the 1920s challenged professional economists writing or advising on policy issues to rethink the nature of the problems facing them and to re-examine some of the basic assumptions of their discipline. Theoretical abstractions and analytical conventions which had fitted so conveniently in the tool-box of the 'new' economic science of the pre-war decades failed to sharpen their focus on the rapid succession of unexpected problems thrown up by a chronically unstable politico-economic environment. Theories of production and exchange which started from the assumption that perfectly competitive markets were the 'norm' had limited relevance to a world in which the restraints on competition were becoming more numerous and effective. The essentially long-term character of classical monetary theory had diminished its usefulness as a frame of reference for analysis of the urgent short-term problems in which most economic decisions have to be made. Most important of all, altering the context in which economic ideas were developing was an ideological shift—a change in the climate of political opinion concerning the proper role of government in economic affairs.

There were two distinct strands in the developing role of government in the twentieth century. The first, which could be called the welfare strand, reflected a tendency for national democratic governments to accept a measure of responsibility for redistributing incomes in favour of the poor and providing welfare services for the underprivileged. The second was the propensity for highly centralized governments to intervene directly in the market system in order to promote national economic power, or prosperity, or to stabilize prices or incomes; that was the social engineering strand. The welfare strand, which culminated in the establishment of the twentieth-century welfare state, has a long history. There was nothing new about the proposition that it was the duty of central government to protect the poor and the weak against economic oppression by the rich and the powerful members of society. True, nineteenth-century classical and neo-classical economists were prone to argue on economic (and Darwinian) grounds that over-protection of the weaker agents in the economic system would diminish their natural propensity to respond productively to market challenges, and so would erode the size of the overall cake in which rich and poor must share. But the steady expansion in central government's welfare functions was an inevitable concomitant of modern industrialization, especially in countries where the franchise was being extended to the under-privileged majority.

Given that some redistribution of incomes through public finance was an accepted objective of government; the problem posed for the new breed of economic scientist was clear: to evolve relevant criteria of economic efficiency and justice by applying the marginal techniques of analysis to alternative forms of public expenditure and taxation. As Pigou, Marshall's successor in the Cambridge chair of political economy, recognized on the occasion of his inaugural lecture: '. . . in the twentieth century the unemployed cannot be allowed to starve.' Accordingly, his first major research project laid the basis for a new branch of economics—welfare economics—by systematically exploring the private and social benefits and costs that might flow from alternative private welfare policies. The message of Pigou's *Wealth and Welfare* (1910—later reissued under the title *Economics of Welfare*)—was that it was possible, *in principle*, purposefully to redistribute income in favour of the poorest groups of society without actually eroding total national product. In practice there is no evidence that Pigou's analysis had any influence at all on the gradual liberalization of social policy that characterized the inter-war period. Indeed, welfare economics developed an increasingly abstract and elaborate theoretical framework in subsequent decades and remained a somewhat esoteric branch of the discipline, at least until after the Second World War when policy-makers began to use cost-benefit calculations in making choices between alternative development expenditures.

It was the other aspect of the changing role of the State—the increasing propensity for central governments to extend the scope of their interventions in capitalist market economies—that was most significant in reshaping economic thought in the twentieth century. For it was here that the really dramatic interactions between economic events, theories and policies took place. Of course increased welfare expenditures played their part in adding to the sheer weight of overall government expenditure and in enlarging the scope for intervention at the macro-economic level. In the four years preceding 1914, total public authorities' expenditure on goods and services and on gross fixed capital formation, plus injections into private sector purchasing power in the form of subsidies and grants and other transfers, together accounted for roughly 10 per cent of the nation's domestic expenditure at market prices. Inevitably there was a sharp rise in the war years, but—in spite of big cutbacks in defence expenditure from the early 1920s—the government's share did not again fall below 16 per cent. By the quadrennium preceding the 1939 rearmament boom it had risen to about a fifth of gross domestic expenditure. This represented a marked increase in the extent to which government could (or would) affect the overall level of economic activity simply by altering the pace or level of its normal annual expenditures.

In the event, each of the two world wars constituted a major turning-point, not only in the weight and range of government's contribution to national economic activity, but also in public opinion concerning the desirability of extending the scope of government's interventions in the economic system. In Britain, for example, when the First World War broke out the only example of a public enterprise that was national in scope was the Post Office. There were municipal enterprises in urban areas (mainly concerned with public utilities such as gas, water, electricity, tramways, ferries, etc.); and there were a few army factories which produced about a third of the guns and ammunition and about half of the military or naval uniforms required for the armed forces. The public sector's contribution to tradable output was thus peripheral and exceptional. In the course of the First World War the government set up a variety of *ad hoc* marketing and manufacturing controls and agencies to ensure that all commodities important to the war effort were readily and cheaply obtainable. Inflation was partially suppressed by controls in the deployment of civilian labour, as well as by price control and rationing of certain staple foodstuffs. At the same time—as a kind of pledge to the masses who had suffered the heaviest burdens of the war effort—government assumed explicit responsibility for managing the difficult transition to a peacetime economy. A Ministry of Reconstruction set up in 1917 began to lay the indispensable foundation for post-war economic planning. In effect, the bureaucracy had had a practical course of instruction in economic planning for victory while businessmen, trade unionists, and civil servants had learned to collaborate in its design and implementation.

Significantly, the lessons learned during the war and its aftermath were not such as to convince either the rulers or the ruled of the virtues of a planned economy in peacetime. Policy-makers remained sceptical of the ability of civil servants to operate efficiently in an entrepreneurial capacity. Business men anticipating a post-war boom could not wait to escape from the straitjacket of profit limitations and price controls when the emergency was over. So the extensive wartime apparatus of control was hastily dismantled. Nevertheless, the experience gained in living with centralized measures of economic control had broadened the horizons of public and private decision makers, dissolved the myth that economic planning was totally unworkable in practice, and opened up new trends in public opinion. The workers had had a taste of full employment and—in effect if not in law—of nationalization of certain key industries (such as railways or mines). Collective controls on private enterprise became major objectives of Labour Party policy and could no longer be brushed aside as hare-brained Bolshevik schemes. For public policymakers and their advisers the task of managing the macroeconomic level and content of national economic activity had proved both challenging and instructive. In these respects the ideological climate would never be the same again.

The British economist who responded more imaginatively than any other to the changing climate of economic opinion and who endeavoured to reinterpret the discipline's view of its basic problem-situation, was John Maynard Keynes (1883–1946). The son of J. Neville Keynes (a pupil and colleague of Marshall), young Maynard had taken rather little interest in economics until he began to read the subject in 1905 as part of his broad preparation for the highly competitive Civil Service examination. He took instruction from Marshall (always keen to attract young graduates to his school) as well as from Pigou, and he gained entry to the India Office. Two years later, having acquired first-hand experience of economic policy formation within the ambit of a major government department, Keynes was more than ready to return to academic life. No formal training was then required to qualify for a lecturing appointment in the leading British faculty of economics and in 1908 Keynes was invited back to Cambridge to teach for the Economics Tripos. Even then he continued to spend most of his spare time researching an interest that had derived from his work for the Mathematical Tripos; and the dissertation he submitted for the King's College fellowship to which he was elected in 1909 was on the theory of probability. Nevertheless, at the age of 27, Keynes had sufficient standing among economists to be appointed editor of the *Economic Journal*, and in 1913—the year he published his first monograph, *Indian Currency and Finance*—he became Secretary of the Royal Economic Society. From January 1915 he worked full-time at the Treasury and earned a brilliant reputation as a Whitehall economist. In 1919 he returned to his teaching and research in Cambridge, became Bursar of King's College, and subsequently an active chairman of a major insurance company. No other British economist of his era (and probably none since) has moved with such confidence, high repute, and technical skill between academia, Whitehall, and the City.

As one of the government's chief economic advisers, in charge of all its external borrowing and lending arrangements in the latter years of the war, Keynes was sent to Paris to represent the Treasury at the peace negotiations. When he resigned from that post in 1919, immediately before the formal signing of the Treaty, it was partly because he was exhausted by four years of heavy war work, and partly also because he was frustrated and disheartened by the economic shortsightedness of the savage reparations imposed by Allied politicans on the defeated European powers. Less than six months later he published the first of what he called his 'essays in persuasion', *The Economic Consequences of the Peace* (1919). This passionate, informed, professional indictment (and recipe for revision) of the Treaty established his international reputation as a radical political economist and stylish iconoclast. Over the next two decades he published a succession of timely articles, pamphlets, and speeches applying the analytical skills of a professional economist, the prophetic insights of an experienced observer, and the expository talents of a literary journalist to the economic policy issues of the day. They were not as persuasive as he had hoped and in 1931 he was to look back on them as 'the croakings of a Cassandra who could never influence the course of events in time'. But they were widely read and sufficiently often justified by events to lend a certain cumulative credibility to his diagnoses, if not to his remedies. When international financial crisis and world economic slump hit the already depressed British economy in 1929–32 the baffled politicians needed expert advice. In a letter to Labour Prime Minister, Ramsay Macdonald, Keynes pressed the case for establishing a standing advisory committee of economists in the following terms: 'It may be that Economics is not enough of a science to produce useful fruits. But I think it might be given a trial, and that we might assume for a moment, if only as a hypothesis, that it can be treated like any other science, and ask for qualified scientists in the subject to have their say.'

The suggestion was taken seriously. Labour and National governments, grappling with a bewildering series of economic shocks from 1929 to 1932, invited professional economists to serve on various *ad hoc* advisory bodies. Keynes himself became an influential member of the Macmillan Committee on Finance and Industry (1929–32), the Economic Advisory Council (1929–32), and the Committee on Economic Information (1932–9). He already enjoyed high academic standing and had acquired a general notoriety by publishing his persistent, often devastating, criticisms of government policy in terms designed to be intelligible to say, the cabinet minister or the educated elector. Most of his *Tract on Monetary Reform* (1923), for example, had originally been written for the *Manchester Guardian Commercial Supplement*, where it appeared as a series of articles offering a forceful diagnosis of the post-war inflation problem within the generally accepted framework of the traditional theory of money. Already, however, his analysis was characterized by two distinctively Keynesian features: first, a conviction that it was no longer possible to rely on *automatic* monetary policies to maintain a stable value of money; and second, a sharp focus on the short-term processes of economic change which classical theorizing had tended to gloss over. He was then concerned above all with the need for purposive monetary management, the purpose being to stabilize prices. After listing the socio-economic consequences of changes in the value of money he concluded that:

Inflation is unjust and deflation is inexpedient. Of the two perhaps deflation is, if we rule out exaggerated inflations such as that of Germany, the worse, because it is worse in an impoverished country to provoke unemployment than to disappoint the rentier. But . . . both are evils to be shunned. The individualistic capitalism of today, precisely because it entrusts saving to the individual investor and production to the individual employer, *presumes* a stable measuring-rod of value, and cannot be efficient—perhaps cannot survive—witout one. For these grave causes we must free ourselves from the deep distrust which exists against allowing the regulation of the standard of value to be the subject of *deliberate decisions*.[1]

In 1926, in a pamphlet entitled *The End of Laissez-Faire*, he developed this theme more broadly and, after reviewing the role played in orthodox economic thinking by the doctrine of *laissez-faire*, called for a more realistic perception of the need for government intervention in the modern economic system.[2]

As for the other novel feature of the Keynesian approach to economic analysis—his emphasis on the need to focus on short-term sequences of economic events when formulating policy prescriptions—that was more implicit than explicit in the *Tract*, though it was here that he made the famous reference to 'the long run in which we are all dead' when commenting on the essentially long run validity of the quantity theory of money. But it was the professional rather than the general reader who needed to be persuaded on this score and it was in his *Treatise on Money* (1930), a comprehensive two-volume text reconstructing the pure and applied theory of money, that Keynes formally redefined the task of monetary theory in dynamic terms thus: 'The real task of such a Theory is to treat the problem dynamically, analysing the different elements involved, in such a manner as to exhibit the causal process by which the price-level is determined and the method of transition from one position of equilibrium to another.'[3]

Keynes's *Treatise on Money* was largely overtaken by events. The collapse into global depression of the overseas boom of the 1920s (which came to a head in the 1929 US Stock Exchange crash), and the disintegration of the gold standard system in 1931 under the strains of internationally transmitted financial crises, radically altered the context of policy problems in the capitalist countries. For the United Kingdom, which had laboriously restored gold convertibility in 1925 at an anachronistic pre-war parity, going off gold finally ended the quest for an automatic, apolitical monetary policy. In effect, it forced the Treasury to assume responsibility for deliberate monetary management. Meanwhile, the slump in world trade had intensified the already heavy burden of UK unemployment and put both its balance of payments and central government budget under increasing pressure, thus lending weight to Conservative arguments for a revenue tariff. It was in finally abandoning free trade that British policy-makers broke away most dramatically from orthodox classical and neo-classical economic doctrine.

The economic case for free trade—rooted in Ricardian comparative cost theory and empirically justified by the upsurge of international trade which followed the repeal of the Corn Laws—had transformed an article of liberal political faith into a 'scientific' doctrine. When Keynes spoke to the Liberal Summer School in 1925, he rejected the individualist political philosophy traditionally associated with the doctrine but stood by its economic logic: 'I believe in free trade because, *in the long run and in general*, it is the only policy which is technically sound and intellectually tight.'[4] The parenthesis (italics supplied) was of course crucial, but in March 1931 orthodox public opinion was scandalized when Keynes published an article advocating a general tariff as remedy for a balance of payments crisis on the assumption that the institutional situation was such that devaluation was ruled out. Then a week after the abandonment of the gold standard in September 1931, he again kicked over the traces: 'There are few Englishmen who do not rejoice at the breaking of our gold fetters. We feel that we have at least a free hand to do what is sensible. The romantic phase is over and we can begin to discuss realistically what policy is for the best.'[5] By then, since devaluation had reduced the urgency of the short-term balance of payments problem, he no longer favoured protective measures: 'the immediate question for attention is not the tariff but the currency question'. Such U-turns in policy prescription were difficult for public opinion to swallow. The popular press had fun lampooning Keynes as the 'boneless economist' and the politicians (equally unable to follow the economic logic of his shifting recommendations) dismissed him as an impractical theorist whose advice was worth following only when it coincided with their own political predilections.

It is on the face of it paradoxical that—in spite of the undoubted advances in economic knowledge and in the quality of economic analysis and research—the international community of economists should have been projecting a less convincing public image in the 1930s than their predecessors, the amateur political economists, had enjoyed a century before. Their diminished public authority stemmed partly from two developments inherent in the professionalization of the discipline: the first was its commitment to a systematically objective approach to the research process; the second was its preoccupation with an increasingly sophisticated and/or technical analytical apparatus. Both developments tended to raise barriers of communication between economists and non-economists. Academics in the United Kingdom, United States, Sweden, and elsewhere were responding to economic change by opening up a variety of new perspectives in economic theory—particularly the theories of money and value. This was when the foundations were being laid for new and more relevant theories of imperfect competition, of the firm and of employment, and when a variety of new concepts and ideas (such as indifference curves, multipliers, and liquidity preference) were brought into play. The era was also characterized by remarkable additions to the stock of empirical economic data and by the associated development of powerful tools of quantitative analysis, incuding national income and input–output accounts. At the interface between economic, mathematical, and statistical theory, a new science was taking shape in the 1930s—econometrics.

Not surprisingly, the results of most of this scholarly effort to advance basic economic knowledge was either incomprehensible to the non-specialist or too remote from everyday problems to lend weight to the applied analysis on which economists' policy prescriptions were founded. It would seem, moreover, that when economists abandoned the attempt to establish universal economic truths in order to improve and drive their admittedly imperfect engine of scientific discovery they lost the aura of infallibility that the public expects of its qualified scientists. *A fortiori*, when they applied their analytical expertise in support of policy programmes associated with particular political parties they could make little headway against more simplistic views that were familiar components of popular opinion. In 1929, for example, Keynes and Hubert Henderson, both leading economists, collaborated in an article entitled 'Can Lloyd George Do It?', which was a spirited defence of the Liberal Party's general election pledge to reduce unemployment substantially by a loan-financed programme of public works. 'The Liberal policy', they insisted, 'is one of plain common sense. The Conservative belief that there is some law of nature which prevents men from being employed, that it is "rash" to employ men, and that it is financially "sound" to maintain a tenth of the population in idleness for an indefinite period is crazily improbable.'[6] It was a deliberately rousing polemic and the fact that the UK unemployment rate had been over 20 per cent in the early 1930s gave it undeniable urgency.

The trouble was, however, that neither the politicians nor their official advisers were persuaded that government could in practice do anything useful to reduce unemployment directly. In this they were supported by conventional economic theory—with its underlying assumption of a self-regulating market economy—though not in practice by all orthodox economists, many of whom were well aware of the limitations of formal theory as a basis for short-term policy prescriptions. The effective opposition to public works policies, however, was not right-wing politicians taking their economics from abstract economic theories, but Whitehall and Bank of England mandarins for whom the overriding aims of government economic policy were to maintain the external stability of the currency and to balance the budget. 'It is orthodox Treasury dogma steadfastly held', announced

Churchill in his 1929 Budget speech, 'that whatever might be the political or social advantages, very little additional employment can, in fact, and as a general rule, be created by State borrowing and expenditure.'[7]

The mandarins could and did justify the 'Treasury view' by arguing (in line with traditional economic theory) that since the capital available at a particular point of time was limited, any increase in government borrowing to finance public works schemes could only be achieved by raising interest rates and at the expense of more productive employment-creating investments in the private sector. Its dogmatic force, however, its persistence, even after the abandonment of the gold standard permitted a 2 per cent Bank Rate from 1932 to 1939, suggests that the officials' stance hinged less on abstract reasoning than on practical budgetary considerations. The fact that few orthodox theorists were prepared to reject altogether the possibility that temporary government relief schemes could usefully reduce unemployment during the slump phase of a trade cycle did not tarnish the Treasury view. On the contrary, the pragmatic approach of the Whitehall mandarins carried the kind of conviction that stems from consistency with well-understood and familiar objectives. It was easy enough to believe that loan-financed public works were not only ineffective as a remedy for long standing unemployment but a positive threat to the moral imperative of a balanced budget.

On the other hand, the economists' argument that such schemes could have a multiplier effect on national recovery smacked of sophistry, if not of wishful thinking. Much more plausible was the contention that the one certain road to industrial recovery lay through improvements in productive efficiency which could only be encouraged, never managed, by central government. Accordingly, although there was a marked retreat from *laissez-faire* principles in the 1930s, and an increasing propensity for British governments to intervene in the operations of the capitalist market economy at the micro-economic level, the paramount objectives of government economic policy remained those of preserving the international exchange value of the pound sterling and balancing the budget. In 1932, for example, the

Conservative Chancellor of the Exchequer who introduced the tariff which ended the long British tradition of free trade listed among its objectives: correcting the balance of payments, raising public revenues, promoting import substitution 'by a system of protection systematically applied', encouraging industrial reorganization with a view to raising productivity, and negotiating discriminatory trade bargains with foreign governments in order to boost British exports.

To give force and direction to the intervention process implicit in these policies new central government institutions were created. An Import Duties Advisory Committee assumed the task of enquiring into the situation and prospects of specific industries and of making consequent recommendations for tariff changes which could be implemented by executive order and without recourse to Parliament. An Exchange Equalization Account was established to stabilize the value of sterling while an embargo was put on foreign lending. At the industry level, State intervention was extended to include—besides discriminatory tariffs and direct subsidies through government-sponsored marketing boards—a variety of measures designed to encourage producers to combine and amalgamate in order to restrict competition.

In retrospect it would seem that these developments lent prophetic force to Keynes's 1926 essay on the end of *laissez-faire*, but it is not evident that either policy-makers or their official advisers were aware of the politico-economic significance of their retreat from *laissez-faire*. Their abandonment of traditional economic doctrine in this respect, reflected their responsiveness to the demands of the producers' lobby rather than a radical vision of what constituted the proper agenda of government. Nor were they persuaded either by the abstract theorizing or the shifting policy prescriptions of academic economists who were notorious for being unable to reach a consensus on practical everyday issues.

There was of course a generalized commitment on the part of policy-makers to promote national recovery, but it was too vaguely conceived to have much impact on either the design of policy or the march of events. Even the 'cheap money' policy embodied in a 2 per cent Bank Rate was dictated more by straightforward fiscal objectives—such as reducing the annual burden of national debt interest—than by its expected consequences for the level of investment or of economic activity. In short, the marked increase in the range and degree of government intervention in the UK economy during the 1930s took place piecemeal, lacking either a considered political philosophy or a coherent economic strategy.

Meanwhile, would-be economic scientists continued to adjust their existing heritage of theories and analytical tools to the changing problems of an unstable world economy. Keynes's *Treatise on Money* (1930), for example, had been an attempt to rescue the traditional theory of money from its exclusive focus on long-term equilibrium situations and to make it more relevant to realistic analysis of the practical problems of economic management in countries such as the United Kingdom and the United States. Building on insights already current in academic debates on monetary and trade cycle analysis, Keynes emphasized that investment decisions in developed economies are taken on different motives (and often by different individuals) than are savings decisions. His analysis of the macro-economic consequences for prices and incomes of divergent movements in aggregate savings and aggregate investment brought out the deflationary implications of an excess of savings over investment and the inflationary consequences of an excess of investment over savings.

This led to the conclusion that cyclical fluctuations in prices and money incomes could be contained by applying appropriate monetary policies, in particular by manipulating interest rates in the directions needed to bring savings and investment smoothly into equilibrium. But by the time the *Treatise on Money* was in print he had shifted to a new object of theoretical research. Convinced that the dominant problem for contemporary western societies in the grip of world depression was not how to stablize prices but how to bring about a sustained recovery in aggregate economic activity, he had begun the intensive debate with his academic colleagues that was to provide the grist for his *General Theory of Employment, Interest and Money* (1936). That was when he finally broke away from what he described as 'the *classical* theory of the subject, upon which I was brought up and which dominates the economic thought, both practical and theoretical, of the governing and academic classes of this generation as it has for a hundred years past'.[8]

The problem with the classical theory was that it was irreconcilable both with the empirical fact of a persistently high level of unemployment and with the public works relief projects that were being seriously discussed, not only by Keynes himself, but by a number of leading economists in the UK, who were far from iconoclastic in their attitudes to economic orthodoxy. The message of orthodox theory was that a long-run tendency to full employment was built in to the competitive market economy by flexible prices and wages which ensured that unemployed workers competing for jobs would pull down wages, raise profits, and thus provide incentives for the new private investment needed to raise the demand for labour. The corollary was that the faster wages were adjusted in a downward direction, the more rapidly would the economic system escape from industrial depression. Against this scenario, however, it could be argued that in the short run the immediate effect of a fall in wage-earners' incomes would be to reduce consumer demand, and hence discourage private investment.

This was the dilemma which Keynes set out to resolve in his *General Theory* by persuading his fellow economists to follow him in shifting their theoretical focus from the factors determining the price level to 'the forces which determine changes in the scale of output and employment as a whole'. From this new perspective he claimed to be able to integrate the 'fundamental theory of value' with the theory of money, so creating a *general* theory of the demand and supply for aggregate real output. The classical theory then fell into place, according to Keynes, as a special case whose characteristics 'happen not to be that of the economic society in which we actually live, with the result that its teaching is misleading and disastrous if we attempt to apply it to the facts of experience'.[9]

Keynes's *General Theory* was thus intended to reconstruct the existing theories of employment and of money so as to make them more relevant to his up-dated reformulation of the problems facing western capitalist economies. There were two salient features of his reconstruction that carried revolutionary analytical implications: first, it adopted an over-arching macro-economic perspective in place of the micro-economic analysis which constituted the nub of classical (and even more of neo-classical) theorizing; and second, it took explicit account of a fact of life conventionally ignored by traditional microtheory—that entrepreneurial decisions are typically based on a fluctuating, vague, and uncertain knowledge of the future. These departures from orthodoxy led him to drop the traditional, if tacit, assumption that every individual spends the whole of his annual income on either consumption or investment goods (Say's Law, which assumed away hoarding) and to develop a theory of money which hinged on its function as a store of wealth when the future seemed uncertain. In effect, once it was recognized that incomes paid out in the production process are not automatically converted into a demand for its outputs, and that investment decisions are confused by incomplete knowledge and uncertain expectations, it was no longer reasonable to regard the economic system as automatically self-regulating in the long run or unemployment as an essentially temporary or frictional problem.

So, having reformulated the problems for economic theory and having brought its starting assumptions closer to contemporary reality, Keynes proceeded in the *General Theory* to construct a macro-economic model of the economic system which could explain variations in the volume of employment. The ultimate determinants of the level of economic activity could be reduced, Keynes postulated, to the following short list of economic variables:

(1) The three fundamental psychological factors, namely the psychological propensity to consume, the psychological attitude to liquidity and the psychological expectation of future yield on capital assets, (2) the wage unit as determined by the bargains reached between employers and the employed, and (3) the quantity of money as determined by the action of the central bank.[10]

These were the explanatory variables which underpinned his innovative approach to the distinctive problems then confronting advanced capitalist economies. He argued, for example, that in relatively developed societies the propensity to save tended to be strong (due to a high average income), while producers' expectations of yield on capital investment tended to be weak (due to the prevailing high level of capital stock). Taken together these psychological attitudes to saving and investment exerted a downward pressure on the level of demand for both consumption and capital goods, thus further weakening the entrepreneurial inducement to invest in situations of uncertainty. The corollary was that the flow of effective demand was unlikely to assume the proportions needed to maintain a full employment level for economic activity, unless exogenous factors intervened (such as a rise in export demand), or unless public expenditures could be strategically used to plug the gap left by the private sector's excess of savings over investment.

Equally revolutionary in its analytical and policy implications was the way Keynes's macro-economic model effectively turned the traditional theory of saving and investment on its head. In classical and neo-classical theory it was the annual savings of those who had a surplus over their current consumption requirements which funded the investment on which that year's real national income (or level of economic activity) depended. The balance between the supply of savings available in a given year, and the demand for investment finance, was adjusted by changes in the long term rate of interest. In this system, given a relatively high propensity to save on the part of the rich, a high level of economic activity was favoured by an unequal distribution of incomes. In Keynes's model, however, the demand for investible funds depended on producers' expectations of the probable return on new investment, while the supply depended on savers' willingness to put their surplus into long-term investments, that is, on their liquidity preference. So, when the prospects for investment seemed uncertain, the long-term rate of interest which would be high enough to persuade savers to part with liquidity could be too high to induce producers to plan new capital formation. This line of argument led Keynes to assert 'that in contemporary conditions the growth of wealth, so far from being dependent on the abstinence of the rich . . . is more likely to be impeded by it'.[11] It also justified an explanation for persistently high unemployment (in terms of a failure of aggregate effective demand) which did not involve the unlikely implication of classical micro-economic analysis that, in so far as unemployment was not due to temporary frictional or structural causes, it was attributable to an obstinate refusal on the part of unemployed labourers to accept a reduction in money wages.

Again, the most significant and revolutionary feature of Keynesian macro-economic analysis lay in the beneficent role it indicated for direct government intervention in the modern market economy. The *Treatise on Money* had stressed the need to adopt monetary policies aimed at managing the value of the national currency and by the 1930s the British monetary authorities had been forced by circumstances to accept responsibility for active monetary management. The *General Theory* went much further by suggesting that government should deliberately deploy the instruments of fiscal and monetary policy with the object of stimulating demand when that was inadequate to absorb the available labour supply, and to restrain it when the factors of production were so fully employed that inflationary pressures were beginning to spiral. It was the idea of systematic demand management that proved most indigestible for orthodox theorists, brought up in a tradition which had abstracted from problems of uncertainty and short-term disequilibria by postulating a model of the competitive exchange economy with a natural long run tendency to equilibrium.

The immediate reception for the *General Theory* by the professionals whom it was intended to convince was highly critical and often hostile. Very few of those who were senior enough to be invited to review it in the learned journals were disposed to follow the author in the 'long struggle of escape from habitual modes of thought and expression' which he demanded of them. Yet, a decade later, when Keynes died, the international community of economists were agreed that there had been a 'Keynesian revolution' in economic ideas.

The first undergraduate text to bring the Keynesian macro-economic perspective to the forefront (in effect by starting its exposition with national income analysis) was John Hicks's *The*

Social Framework (1941), appearing five years after the *General Theory* itself. Not surprisingly, the younger generation of economists found it easier to identify with the new macro-economics than did their elders. Paul Samuelson, for example, who had been in his early twenties when the debate hit the USA, was inclined in retrospect to recollect the experience in a spirit of 'bliss was it in that dawn to be alive'. His elementary textbook (first published in 1947) dominated undergraduate teaching of economics for at least a generation, and like its many imitators gave precedence to Keynesian macro-economics in expounding the discipline to beginners. But even some of those who had been Keynes's most influential antagonists in the 1930s—such as Lionel Robbins of the London School of Economics, or Pigou, whose *Theory of Unemployment* had been the favourite scapegoat in the *General Theory's* assault on classical orthodoxy, readily acknowledged when the obituaries were written in 1946 the breakthrough achieved by the new macro-economics. No other work in economic theory had had such a rapid and stimulating effect on the way economists approached economic problems or developed their research or teaching programmes.

9

The rise and fall of
economic management

> Cock-sure certainty is the source of much that is worst in
> our present world, it is something of which the contem-
> plation of history ought to cure us, not only chiefly
> because there were wise men in the past, but because so
> much that was thought wisdom turned out to be folly—
> which suggests that much of our supposed wisdom is no
> better.
>
> Bertrand Russell

The proliferating army of twentieth-century economists serving
as academic teachers or researchers or as popularizers of
economic ideas, or as advisers to economic policy-makers in
government or business, were faced—more often and more dis-
concertingly than their predecessors—with the need to adapt
their specialized learning and analytical equipment to perpetually
changing problems. When Keynes wrote his *General Theory of
Employment, Interest and Money* (1936) it was to provide a
coherent theoretical framework within which to analyse the
problems of a modern capitalist economy suffering from chronically high under-employment of labour and capital. By 1937, the
Great Depression was over and the world economy had reached a
new output peak with manufacturing production roughly double
the pre-First World War high. In Britain, unemployment was
down to 10.8 per cent of the insured population (not yet down to
the 1929 low) while regional disparities had widened, so that the
rate was still over 22 per cent in Wales and nearly 16 per cent in
Scotland. By then the Committee on Economic Information was
persuaded by Keynes that the British unemployment problem
was best regarded as a regional rather than a national one. The
corollary was that except in the specially depressed areas of the

north and west, government should now be advised to postpone rather than expand public investment in roads and housing, for example, until the downswing of the trade cycle was clearly under way again. In the event, cyclical recovery was prolonged through 1938 and 1939 by a rearmanent boom which culminated in the Second World War.

For the second time within a quarter of a century, the onset of war radically transformed the problems facing governments and did so in ways that lent immediate relevance to the distinctively macro-economic management approach advocated by Keynes and his disciples. Hitherto (at least until the 1938–9 rearmanent programme) the UK Treasury had kept faith with its balanced budget principles. Certainly it had refused to follow the example of some leading western governments (including the USA, France, Sweden, and Germany) which had deliberately financed industrial recovery by running up budget deficits. But from October 1939 onwards the objective of victory over-rode all others, and those responsible for government economic policies became increasingly receptive to Keynes's advice on how to finance the war.

In memoranda aimed directly at the UK Treasury, as well as in a series of articles for *The Times* in late 1939—subsequently published in a pamplet entitled *How to Pay for War* (1940)—Keynes advocated a budget strategy designed to minimize inflationary pressures inherent in war expenditures by adjusting public receipts and expenditures to the expected levels of overall national demands on resources. In June 1940 he was appointed to the Consultative Committee set up to advise the Chancellor, and the beginnings of a Keynesian revolution in UK economic policy making were signalled in the latter's Budget Speech which developed the macro-economic argument of an inflationary gap between aggregate demand and aggregate supply to justify a radical new tax scheme.

It was thus the war which created the political climate for Keynes to realize his ambition to 'revolutionize the way the world thinks about economic problems'. The inflationary gap argument was in essence very simple. It was that an excess of war-inflated demand over supply would cause prices to spiral upwards unless the expected gap could be narrowed by a corresponding reduction of consumers' purchasing power. More remarkable was the way the macro-economic reasoning was used to underpin a new tax proposal. For part of the tax to be raised from consumers to cover the following year's war expenditures was designated a 'post-war credit', to be repaid in peacetime when the expected contraction in government expenditures raised the spectre of a postwar slump.

There, in the 1941 Budget proposals, lay the seed of the British government's explicit commitment (in peace as in war) to a demand management stance, i.e. to manipulating its fiscal receipts and payments in such a way as to restrain demand when it was expected to be excessive and to stimulate it when it appeared deficient. Before the end of 1941, the numbers unemployed had fallen below 200,000 and the rapid disappearance of all but frictional levels of unemployment seemed to demonstrate the overwhelming importance of a high level of public sector expenditure in determining the overall level of economic activity. It also made the prospect of a return to the high unemployment levels typical of inter-war experience politically unacceptable—particularly to the younger generation of government economic advisers for whom Keynes's *General Theory* had been a potent source of inspiration.

The war also stimulated a national statistical research programme to provide for the relatively large and mounting data needs of macro-economic policy makers. The Central Statistical Office paper *Estimates of National Income and Expenditure 1938–41 and Analysis of the Sources of War Finance*, published to document the accounting framework underlying the 1941 Budget strategy, was the first in an annual series of United Kingdom national accounts. Not surprisingly the data series started then mirrored the theoretical concepts and modelling conventions developed in the *General Theory*. By this means the now extensive and numerous intellectual community of those concerned with contemporary economic questions—from politicians and civil servants to financial journalists, from bankers and businessmen to trade unionists, from academic theorists to their undergraduate pupils—became familiar with the empirical counterparts of the Keynesian abstractions. They soon learned to deploy the strategic propositions of Keynesian macro-economic analysis in discussing economic trends and policies and to do so with a greater facility and conviction than most of them would have had for orthodox micro-economic analysis. Meanwhile, for technically sophisticated graduate students who provided the recruits to a small but growing élite of research economists, the close association of a new and coherent system of economic theory with a relative abundance of up-to-date empirical data encouraged the pursuit of 'scientific' research programmes in what it became fashionable to refer to as positive economics.

Keynes himself remained wholly committed to policy-orientated enquiries during the war years, though he held no full-time position in the official hierarchy. As an acknowledged expert who enjoyed outstanding international repute and professional influence, he moved naturally into the role of a mainly freelance consultant who was as ready to offer advice to American as to British policy-makers and to exchange views with journalists or trade unionists as with academic theorists or civil servants. His disciples, however, were multiplying—no longer merely among the younger generation of economists who, being (as he described it) 'not properly brought up', were more open to unorthodox ideas than their elders. In these circumstances, in the abnormal context of total war, the Keynesian approach to economic analysis began to predominate and to develop on lines that were not always directly attributable to the master. The select group of academic economists serving as temporary civil servants in the Economic Section of the UK Cabinet Office, for example, assumed the quintessentially Keynesian concern with post-war employment policy from 1941 onwards, while Keynes himself was largely preoccupied with pressing questions of war finance or with devising plans for a post-war international economic order.

Once full employment had been reached (passed indeed) it no longer seemed an unattainable object to set before post-war governments. There was of course a problem of defining the target. In 1944 the total numbers seeking work in Britain had fallen to roughly 75,000 out of a total labour force of over 22 million people. On the face of it, the 3 per cent level then proposed in *Full*

Employment in a Free Society (1944) by Sir William Beveridge—whose long-standing credentials as an expert on the unemployment problem were unquestionable—seemed a modest enough target to postulate in public debates on the issue. True, neither the officials nor their Keynesian advisers were as optimistic as Beveridge in their estimates of what might be a feasible level for a 'free society', once the extensive physical and other wartime controls on private consumption and incomes policies had been lifted. The 1944 White Paper on Employment Policy (rushed out just weeks ahead of Beveridge's much-heralded monograph) avoided nomination of a specific full employment target, for example, and pointed to the inflationary pressures likely to be generated by demand mangement policies aimed at minimizing unemployment. Nevertheless, the White Paper made political history, raising the sights of the British electorate by committing its government to maintenance of a 'high and stable level of employment' as a major objective.

A similar commitment was accepted by the US Federal government in the 1946 Employment Act. In the United Kingdom events actually exceeded the most optimistic expectations. For only one of the next twenty five years did the annual percentage unemployment rate rise close to the 3 per cent level and that was in the wholly abnormal fuel crisis year of 1947. Before the end of the 1940s it looked as though the systematic application of demand management techniques would suffice to keep the average annual unemployment percentage and the long-term rate of inflation down to politically acceptable levels. Accordingly, most of the direct wartime controls focused on these objectives were consigned to a bonfire of controls at the end of 1948 and the British experiment in demand management went into top gear.

At that stage the problem of maintaining the internal stability of the United Kingdom economy almost seemed reducible to a mainly technical matter of forecasting predictable movements in national demand and supply aggregates and adopting the appropriate fiscal policy stance to keep them in balance. External stability was more problematic, however, in view of the acute balance of payments disequilibria facing not only the United

Kingdom but most other national economies involved in the difficult transition from war to peace.

As was dramatically illustrated by the badly co-ordinated devaluations of 1949 and by the international spillover effects of inflationary pressures generated by the Korean War, the prospects of effectively stabilizing prices and economic activity in the United Kingdom (as elsewhere) were tightly constrained by world trends and events. Indeed, one of the hard-learned lessons that had emerged forcibly from the inter-war experience was that a disorderly international monetary system would certainly jeopardize attempts to implement a consistent set of domestic economic policies. As early as 1942, therefore, the British and American governments had set their economic experts to collaborate in devising a viable set of rules, conventions, and institutions governing the way the leading trading nations should be persuaded to conduct their economic relations with the rest of the world. In that initial planning process Keynes played a major part, particularly in relation to the international monetary system. Although the Agreement reached at Bretton Woods in 1944 came closer in some respects to the proposals advocated by his American counterparts than to his own, the underlying rationale reflected his personal vision of the need to establish new 'rules of the game' that were comparable with, but more flexible than, those of the pre-1914 gold standard. The basic assumption was that nations seeking to get on a path of steady economic growth could achieve their aims only within the context of an external monetary environment that was generally perceived to be both expansive and stable.

To this global purpose the Bretton Woods Agreement set up two new international organizations: (1) the International Monetary Fund, designed to maintain stability of the foreign exchanges by enabling participating countries to ride out short-term balance of payments problems; and (2) the International Bank for Reconstruction and Development (later generally known as the World Bank), designed to facilitate the movement of surplus long-term investment funds to countries with the most urgent development needs.

It was not until the mid-1950s that the IMF was strong enough to inject an appreciable measure of stability into the international monetary system. However, its rules stipulated that each member country should establish a fixed par value for its currency in terms either of gold or of the US dollar, departing from that value only when it faced a 'fundamental disequilibrium' in its balance of payments rectifiable by adjusting to a new fixed exchange value. Countries faced with less radical balance of payments problems were to be helped to maintain the value of their currency by automatic access to Fund resources up to the limit of a pre-set quota and on accepting increasingly stringent conditions of internal monetary discipline beyond that limit. The World Bank got into its stride a little earlier than the IMF and was able to channel investment capital readily to war-torn Western Europe from the late 1940s and to underdeveloped third world countries from the early 1950s.

The other aspect of the post-war international order on which qualified economists serving wartime governments could claim to offer expert advice to planners was on the need to scale down the heavy crust of protectionism built up in the 'beggar-your-neighbour' climate of the depressed 1930s. Here again the political prerequisite was to persuade those countries which accounted for a significant proportion of world imports and exports to agree on an appropriate code of conduct. Accordingly, in 1947, the General Agreement on Tariffs and Trade established another new international organization, designed to steer participating countries towards a multilateral, non-discriminatory approach to international trade policies. By the end of 1951 the signatories to GATT accounted for more than 80 per cent of world trade and had jointly negotiated substantial tariff reductions.

Thereafter, although the range and pace of advance in tariff concessions slowed down markedly, GATT continued to act as a pressure point for further trade liberalization, particularly among the relatively developed countries of the world and in relation to manufactured goods. The non-discriminatory ideal which had once seemed the most fundamental of GATT aims proved less compelling in practice to subsequent policy-makers than it had appeared in principle to the original signatories. Nevertheless, the various regional (or political) trade groupings that took shape in the 1950s—including for example the

Organization for European Economic Co-operation (Western Europe plus the USA and Canada), the Council for Mutual Economic Assistance (covering the Soviet dominated countries of Eastern Europe), the European Common Market (1957), the European Free Trade Association (for western European countries not in the EEC)—had beneficial if limited, trade-liberalizing effects for most of the relatively developed countries of the world.

The reconstructed economic order of the post-Second World War era may not have fulfilled the highest hopes of the economists involved in planning for it, but the contrast with the chaotic aftermath of the First World War is striking. A combination of economic co-operation and political competition set the tone of international economic relations. From 1947, when the government of the dominant national economy, the United States, launched the Marshall Plan—a massive aid programme supplying war-devastated countries with scarce agricultural and manufactured goods—the world economy's recovery from inter-war depression and wartime structural distortion was rapid and sustained. It was the start of a golden age in which rates of growth in national income per head reached historically high levels for over two decades in developed and underdeveloped countries, in market and socialist economies alike. How much of this upsurge in world trade, incomes, and productivity was due to the new spirit of the age reflected in the virtually universal commitment of national governments to promoting high levels of economic activity and faster growth rates, and how much to the existence of the new international order, is debatable. Certainly world trade expanded faster than world output. More interestingly, and possibly more significant, however, is that a newly optimistic spirit inspired the constitutions of the new institutions set up to structure and monitor the strategic inter-country relationships in the post-war era. Article I of the Constitution of the International Monetary Fund, for example, listed among its purposes: 'to facilitate the expansion and balanced growth of international trade, and to contribute thereby to the promotion and maintenance of high levels of employment and real income and to the development of the productive resources of all members as primary objectives of economic policy'. During this golden age, frequently cited as a vindication of the Keynesian revolution in economic ideas, the popular reputation of the professional economist reached an all-time peak.

In the United Kingdom, where the Keynesian tradition was strongest, the three decades following the outbreak of the Second World War have been conventionally labelled the 'age of economic management'. Certainly there had been a major shift of attitudes by comparison with the post-1918 era when informed observers typically concluded from their wartime experience (backed by orthodox economic theory) that systematic government intervention in a peacetime market economy was unlikely to produce efficient results. By the 1940s, public opinion was ready to embrace the notion that well-designed macro-economic policies were capable of steering the economy towards nationally agreed objectives; and the economics profession had developed a high degree of confidence in its capacity to offer useful advice on how it should be done. What was different, however, about economic management, once the war was over, was that it focused on multiple objectives—not simply on the overriding aim of military victory or the more abstract utilitarian aim of maximizing general welfare.

Four specific economic objectives were commonly invoked by the UK and other western governments after the Second World War. They were: stable prices, a satisfactory balance of payments, full employment and a rate of economic growth that matched the contemporary performance of other advanced economies. The last two of these represented additions to the traditional agenda of government. When full employment and economic growth were added to the menu of government responsibilities it soon became obvious that the problem with a multiplicity of objectives was not simply the political one of reconciling the divergent priorities that major sections of the community (or major political parties) assigned to generally agreed aims. It was that each economic objective called for a package of policy instruments with conflicting or complementary implications for the other objectives. Nor, as it turned out, were the policy instruments themselves politically neutral elements in economic strategy. Indeed, commitment to a particular shade in the political spectrum was often associated with strong preferences for or against specific instruments.

During the early post-war years, when the UK rate of economic growth was riding on the back of an export-led boom, at roughly twice the pace it had reached in the pre-war quinquennium, conflict between the leading macro-economic objectives hardly showed. Bank Rate stood at 2 per cent until 1951; investment was buoyant and unemployment low, if variable; while the rate of inflation compared favourably with that of most other developed countries. From 1951, however, in spite of a substantial devaluation of the pound sterling in 1949, a succession of balance of payments crises effectively limited attempts to prevent the long-term unemployment rate from rising. The growth objective rose to prominence after the mid-1950s, when it became plain that although the UK rate of growth was still historically high, it lagged persistently behind that of most other industrial countries. It was then that the 'age of management' degenerated into the era of 'stop–go'. Each attempt to expand the growth rate by the conventional Keynesian recipe of reflating demand increased expenditure on imports and made it easier for potential exporters to sell at home, thus precipitating a balance of payments disequilibrium. Given their obligation to fix the exchange rate, the authorities were then forced to adopt deflationary measures which put brakes on growth. Far from stabilizing the national level of economic activity, demand management generated a succession of stop-go cycles, with deeply disappointing implications for the long-term growth rate.

On the face of it, the fact that the annual rate of unemployment did not exceed 3 per cent until the 1970s argues some success for UK demand management in relation to what was originally its most important objective. But at each deflationary downturn of the stop-go sequence the numbers unemployed crept to a higher level than in the last. More alarming still was a tendency which was built into the sellers' market for labour and heightened by the presence of a militant, decentralized trade union movement. By 1961 the government was sufficiently concerned by the impact of rising wage costs on the international competitiveness of UK manufacturing industry to add an incomes policy to the package of instruments which it deployed against the current balance of payments crisis. By 1967 it had been driven to devalue the pound. The problem of rising wage costs pushing up prices was by no means unique to the United Kingdom, but for a variety of structural and institutional reasons it was there that it first began to assume significant dimensions in the calculations of economic policy makers and to set challenging problems for economic theorists.

Given the upward drift of unemployment rates in the down phases of the stop-go cycle and of inflation rates in the up phases, it was not surprising that the new Keynesian orthodoxy (in Britain as in the United States) chose to analyse the evident incompatibility between stable prices and full employment as a trade-off problem: how far was it possible to move in the direction of one objective without sacrificing a conflicting objective to an unacceptable extent? No doubt this perspective was influenced by the professional myopia which encourages economists to focus on the economic causes of socio-economic processes such as inflation, to the neglect of, say sociological or institutional factors. So when in 1958, Professor A. W. Phillips of the London School of Economics published the results of his empirical investigation into 'the relation between unemployment and the rate of change of money wage rates in the United Kingdom in 1861–1957', it set the mould of economic debate and of research on the causes of inflation for over a decade.[1]

The manifest weakness of the historical statistics on which the article hinged did not prevent it from being welcomed by many economists as a convincing demonstration that excess demand for labour was a sufficient explanation for the tendency of money earnings to rise ahead of productivity and to inject a wage–cost-push element into the current inflationary process. A spate of empirical studies appeared in the learned journals to confirm the existence in other countries of the Phillips curve (that is, of an inverse relationship between money wage inflation and unemployment). The methodological and data deficiencies identified by researchers who commented critically on these statistical exercises were of interest only to specialists. On the other hand, the trade-off reasoning implicit in the Phillips curve was of wide general interest and it rapidly passed into common currency as part of the economists' standard tool-kit for analysing inflation.

The extreme simplicity of the underlying hypothesis guaranteed its popularity as an analytical tool. For what politicians (and educated opinion generally) demand from the economic experts are easily intelligible, empirically defensible, and readily applicable policy criteria. The Phillips curve, for example, was to give rise to the neat 'rule of thumb' that when unemployment rates fell below 2 per cent the appropriate response to rising money wage rates was to restrain aggregate demand: if they were between 2 and 2.25 per cent a wages policy could offer a useful alternative to even tighter fiscal or monetary deflation; above a 2.25 per cent unemployment rate the wage-push pressure was unlikely to have cumulative consequences and it would then be appropriate to relax demand constraints in order to counter a further threatened rise in unemployment.[2]

Two crucial assumptions underlay the deployment of the Phillips curve in analyses of inflation during the 1960s. The first was that it accurately identified the strategic variables in the inflation mechanism. The second was that it depicted a stable relationship, even if its precise measurements must be expected to differ as between countries and also over time when radical institutional changes occurred. The first of these assumptions was questioned by certain economic theorists as well as by social scientists unable to credit that the non-economic factors in inflation were of negligible importance in practice. The second assumption was undermined by events in the late 1960s and early 1970s when unemployment, wage rates, and inflation each showed an upward trend and policy makers were confronted by a problem not predicted by orthodox Keynesian analysis—the problem of stagflation.

A reaction against the Keynesian revolution in economic theory was already in evidence in the mid-1950s, before the Phillips curve article appeared. Neither Keynes nor the Keynesian succession had deviated from basic classical theory at the micro-level of analysis, with the result that a tension persisted in the post-war textbooks between a body of macro-economic theory starting from the assumption that 'free' markets do not always clear in the short run and a body of micro-economic theory starting from the assumption that they always clear in the long run. The tension was as much political as methodological in character for it reflected the perennial conflict between interventionist and *laissez-faire* views of the role of the state in economic affairs.

Significantly, what was later called the 'monetarist counter revolution' originated in the University of Chicago, where a vigorous tradition of liberal individualism created a fertile environment for the development of economic theories justifying market solutions to economic policy problems. It was spearheaded in 1956 by Milton Friedman's restatement of the quantity theory of money, rejection of which had been at the heart of the heresy contained in Keynes' *General Theory*.[3] As is often true of theoretical controversies in economics, the protagonists' choice of assumptions determined not only the field of battle, and the analytical time reference, but also the conflicting policy implications. Thus Friedman's restatement of the quantity theory in terms appropriate to a modern capitalist economy started from a classical focus on the long-term sequence of cause and effect in an economy with a natural tendency to adjust to an equilibrium (that is, to a situation in which all participants in the market are satisfied with their own current position). He further postulated: (1) that the demand for money is a stable function of the level of income and the volume of transactions, and (2) that the supply of money is exogenously determined (by the monetary authorities rather than by market behaviour of individuals). Starting from these assumptions it was easy to infer that 'inflation is always and everywhere a monetary problem' and that government action to reduce the level of unemployment by loan-financed spending programmes must be self-defeating *in the long run* because the associated increase in the money supply would create inflation.

What is most interesting and significant about the Keynesian/monetarist controversy is that the protagonists were armed by two lively, competing macro-economic research programmes, each of which promised (and went on to deliver) advances in economic knowledge on both its empirical and theoretical frontiers. Because they adopted divergent starting assumptions, leading to different models of the way the economic system operated, and also because they focused on differing specifications of economic problems to which both attached high priority, it was not a competition in which either approach could be seen to be on a winning route to objective economic truth or in which it was reasonable to suppose that the eventual outcome of their critical confrontations would be a consensus.

Of course, to the extent that their conceptual building blocks were similar and the connecting mechanisms they postulated were empirically (and unambiguously) testable, their researches and counter-criticims did result in a measure of agreement on certain matters of fact that had been hotly disputed. On the other hand, the initial empirical hypotheses built into competing models of the economic system are necessarily too simplified, too stylized, to be conclusively falsified by new sets of observations, even where the latter are sufficiently well established to command general acceptance. For example, time series showing a high correlation between the stock of money in circulation and the level of prices are as consistent with the monetarist assumption that the direction of causation typically runs from an exogenously determined money supply to the rate of inflation as with the Keynesian belief that it often runs from an exogenously determined rise in, say, wage rates or imported commodity costs to an induced demand for credit to finance a higher nominal value of output.

At the theoretical level the new perspectives and insights opened up by the competition between alternative macro-economic doctrines were occasionally more fruitful. In the debates on the Phillips curve, for example, Friedman succeeded in undermining the Keynesian vision of the relationship as one illustrating a trade-off between conflicting demand management objectives, by respecifying it in terms of real rather than money wage rates. Making the realistically plausible assumption that in the modern labour market both sides in the wage bargain take the expected rate of inflation into account, he brought the dynamic concept of inflationary expectations into the analysis of inflation and unemployment. This enabled the monetarist to offer an intelligible explanation (within his distinctive package of assumptions) for the problem of stagflation dominating the 1970s when inflation and unemployment defied the prediction implicit in the Keynesian model and rose together. The monetarist interpretation was that in a situation where wage bargains are negotiated in the expectation of continuously rising prices, real wage costs (and hence unemployment) will tend to rise unless actual inflation exceeds anticipated inflation. Hence active demand management policies designed to reduce unemployment can only succeed by pushing up inflation rates.

Of course the idea of taking account of inflationary expectations in analysing market behaviour has obvious relevance beyond the Phillips curve debate and was destined to stimulate a modern macro-economic research programme founded on pre-Keynesian assumptions. What has been called the 'new classical macro-economics', for example, assumes that market agents behave rationally in maximizing their ends, that they learn from experience to form the best expectations possible with the information at their disposal and that free markets are constantly clearing—or are in equilibrium. In short, by building on the traditional principles of classical micro-economic theory, the new doctrine overcame the tensions between orthodox micro- and orthodox macro-economics which were the heritage of the Keynesian Revolution and brought into sharp focus the hitherto neglected question of how in practice expectations inform and guide market behaviour in a changing environment.

The role of intellectual controversy in advancing scientific knowledge is well known and does not need emphasis here. However, the pervasive policy orientation which distinguishes most debates on political economy sheds doubts on the objectivity of critique and counter-critique. Among the policy conclusions drawn from (and indeed written into the assumptions of) the monetarist research programme, for example, were: (1) that demand management policies aimed at reducing unemployment would eventually and inevitably raise both inflation and unemployment; and (2) that the only macro-economic policy likely to prove effective against inflation was that of controlling the money supply on clearly publicized, automatic (non-discretionary) rules designed to keep it in line with the expected long-term trend in the volume of transactions.

The conclusions of the 'new classical macro-economics' were even more *laissez-faire* in their implications, for it represented an extension of Adam Smith's invisible hand doctrine from micro-economic to macro-economic levels of analysis. Rational expectations theory, for example, postulates that agents in market economies are primarily concerned to maximize their own self-interest and that market prices are sensitive barometers and indicators of current and prospective economic conditions. On these assumptions, Keynesian demand management policies cannot alter the 'natural' parameters of the economic system set by historical, institutional, and other constraints; they can only make markets operate less efficiently than they would otherwise tend to do, by injecting additional uncertainties and confusions into the information system on which producers base their decisions.

Given that economics is not an exact science, that the operational characteristics of the economic system it seeks to understand vary through time and space, it is neither surprising nor unfortunate that there should exist competing research programmes leading to conflicting policy advice. The policy-makers have choices to make—as also do the researchers seeking a coherent analytical framework for their enquiries. Rational choices between alternative models of the economic system depend on finding the model which most effectively illuminates the central question at issue. There are no all-purpose economic theories. Nevertheless, the fact that differences in the starting assumptions and methodological conventions built into competing research programmes are typically associated with distinctive ideological positions carrying specific policy predilections, ensures that the heat resulting from intellectual confrontations between leading (and equally reputable) economists is more obvious to the non-professional observer than the light. That was one reason why the scientific standing of professional economists slumped in the 1970s from the unwarranted heights it reached in the 1950s and 1960s. The other reason was the challenge of events.

The various experiments in demand management undertaken by the governments of western market economies in the third quarter of the twentieth century demonstrated two lessons of importance for the history of political economy—one primarily economic, the other primarily political. The first was that in the current state of the discipline insufficient understanding and information on the economic system was available to steer it efficiently in pursuit of specific macro-economic goals. The second was that the pursuit of multiple (conflicting or complementary) objectives raises complex socio-political issues of choice, in relation not only to alternative priority systems, but also to the policy instruments used; for there is usually more than one way of approaching a given objective and instruments carry side effects which may conflict with non-economic values such as justice, or freedom, or the quality of life.

Neither management problem was soluble. The problem of inadequate knowledge, for example, was not simply a matter of collecting and processing more and better data or of devising more powerful theories, for neither data nor theories can stay sufficiently abreast of a changing economic system to validate either the short-term decisions that constitute the daily routine of economic management or the longer-term vision needed to define and set acceptable 'rules of the game'. Macro-economic data describe the past rather than the present or future and are in any case incomplete. Even in the case of such a crucial and familiar trigger for short-term policy decisions as, say, the latest balance of payments estimates, it is notoriously difficult to assess the dimensions and causes of a current deficit, or surplus, in time to take appropriate action. It is equally difficult to arrive at timely and reliable estimates of the rate of growth of the money supply—apart altogether from the problem of defining money itself, that is, of drawing a line between 'pure' money and those liquid assets which are so readily convertible into money that they have most of the same properties. Economic theories also have their time limits and a theory that satisfactorily explains yesterday's market behaviour patterns and economic events may positively impede attempts to understand today's or predict tomorrow's. These were some of the lessons of experience drawn from the disappointing results of short-term management policies, or longer-term national plans, by those concerned with their formulation or implementation in the post-war era. Meanwhile, attempts by successive elected governments to grapple with the socio-political discontent sparked off by activist economic policies did more to destabilize the economy (e.g. by generating 'election cycles' in economic activity or legislating for unexpected changes in the 'rules of the game') than they did to stem the mounting public disenchantment with the tax burdens and other constraints on private economic freedom imposed by a massively expanding administrative system.

When the unprecedented (and perhaps unrepeatable) upsurge in world economic growth which characterized the 1950s and 1960s ended in the 1970s, the social and political costs of both the successes and the failures of a high level of government intervention in national and international economic systems were already fanning the flames of a libertarian reaction which had added heat to popular debate, even in the special circumstances of total war. For example, Friedrich von Hayek's *Road to Serfdom* (1944)—a systematic indictment of the drift towards tyranny inherent in socialist policies—was a best seller in wartime England, as well as in Sweden and the USA. It had been translated and reprinted in many European countries before the end of the 1940s and in Japan and China in the 1950s, and it continued to dramatize the post-war critique of 'piecemeal social engineering'. Then, in the late 1960s—when unemployment and inflation rose together in most western countries, when the pace of economic growth faltered in developed and underdeveloped, in market and command economies alike, and when the system of international trade and payments came under increasing strain for a variety of economic and political reasons—Hayek's distinctive economic philosophy, unified by Smith's thesis of a spontaneous social order, offered well-publicized and documented intellectual foundations for a liberal ideological revival.

An evidently decisive break with past economic trends came in 1971 when the United States pulled out the gold peg that was propping up the dollar and the Bretton Woods system. The immediate effect of this shift from a (mainly) fixed to a (mainly) floating exchange rate system was to free participating governments from the burden of having to stifle every major domestic expansion in order to fix the external value of the national currency. The result was a world economic boom leading to an international inflation that threatened to assume catastrophic proportions. Soaring international commodity prices (including a quintupling of the price of oil) plunged the world into industrial recession and fast inflation after the pace of world productivity growth had begun to slow down appreciably. The age of stagflation had begun. The award to Hayek of a Nobel Prize in Economics in 1974 reflected a rising libertarian tide among contemporary academic economists.

While the prevailing orthodoxy conformed to what was generally thought of as Keynesian economics—as it did for most of the 1950s and 1960s—the standard undergraduate introductory text expounded the fundamental principles of the discipline in two compartments. Part I typically described a macro-economic model inspired by Keynes's *General Theory*. Part II presented neo-classical micro-theory leading to the traditional conclusion that, in freely competitive markets, the operations of the price system tend over the long run to maximize aggregate output. This sat uneasily with the Keynesian message that in an uncertain world, effective demand tends to fall short of the level required to bring all available labour and capital into productive use. Since the two areas of theory have to be brought into harness for the purposes of realistic analysis, much sophisticated theorizing was devoted to the problem of harmonizing their logic and implications. In most discussions of macro-economic policy, at least in the early post-war years, a relatively simple solution was widely accepted. It was that so long as governments maintained a fiscal policy stance designed to offset the instabilities of private spending, the price mechanism could be relied upon to fulfil its classical function of bringing aggregate output close to its full employment potential. At that stage the role of monetary policy tended to be regarded as of secondary importance in a demand management strategy.

This perspective on the contemporary economic problems facing developed market economies stimulated a heavy concentration of research effort and debate on the determination and effective control of demand. As events tempered the initial high optimism of the Keynesians concerning the potency of fiscal policy instruments in particular and efficiency of demand management in general they were forced to reconsider (*a*) their views concerning the role of monetary policy, and (*b*) the micro-foundations of their macro-economic models.

The monetarist research programme and critique accordingly attracted increasing interest from both theorists and applied economists, while some of the leading academics turned their attention to developing more rigorous and powerful micro-theories. What finally killed the so-called Keynesian consensus, however, was the succession of destabilizing events that shook the world economy in the early 1970s; in particular, the break-down of the Bretton Woods system, the commodity (especially oil) price explosion, and the sinister coincidence of accelerating inflation and obstinately rising unemployment in all advanced market economies. These shocks exposed the limitations of economic management with dramatic finality. They also reordered the agenda of government in western economies by bringing inflation to the top as the most urgent and alarming contemporary economic problem.

The world inflation of the post-1972 era was a particularly shattering experience for nations with a strong tradition of sound finance and entrenched expectations of essentially stable price levels. In the United Kingdom, for example, inflation soared in the mid-1970s to heights never before reached in peacetime; the annual percentage rise in consumers' prices was near to 24 per cent in 1975 and averaged over 15 per cent through the decade 1974/83. Consumers felt themselves impoverished by such rapid price increases (even when wages were rising faster); producers hesitated to undertake new long-term investments when unable to forecast comparative trends in their costs and selling prices; governments were under fire because their share in gross national product was rising faster than the real value of the services they provided; and all those individuals and groups who needed to plan their incomes and expenditures a year or more ahead found their budgeting practices disoriented by rises in absolute, and shifts in relative, price levels that were both volatile and unpredictable.

Meanwhile fear of runaway inflation—driven by international winds of change and possibly leading to catastrophic hyper-inflation of the kind experienced in some countries after the First World War—haunted responsible observers after the breakdown of the Bretton Woods discipline left currency exchange rates and international financial asset prices at the mercy of speculators and hedgers operating in highly competitive money markets. The sense of economic crisis was profound and-pervasive. It was enhanced by two contemporary circumstances. One was the revolution in information technology asociated with an explosive increase in the size, power, and sophistication of the world's financial markets, which made it increasingly difficult for individual national governments to apply effective direct exchange controls to protect their currencies or their domestic price levels against internationally transmitted inflationary pressures. The second was the manifest inability of the acknowledged economic experts to agree either on the determinants of inflation or on the best ways of controlling it.

Predictably, the reactions of the now very diverse community of professional economists to the crumbling of the Keynesian orthodoxy were various. It discomfited the many practitioners who had basked in the unwarranted credit accruing to the high priests of economic management in the golden age. The generalized sense of professional unease found expression in a spate of 'laments for economics' published in the early 1970s by well-known members of the economic establishment—for example, the Presidents of the American Economic Association, of the Royal Economic Society, and of the Econometric Society, to name only a few of the elder statesmen who castigated economists for claiming more scientific authority for their discipline than it could then (or perhaps ever) deliver. Keynes himself would no doubt have added to the chorus of lament had he survived to see his revolutionary message ossify into an orthodoxy and the relentless procession of 'Keynesian' econometric models grinding out their exact numerical results in the learned journals. His own thrust was towards developing an 'art of political economy' rather than a positive economic science. 'In chemistry and physics and other natural sciences', he had insisted, 'the object of experiment is to fill in the actual values of the various quantities and factors appearing in an equation or formula and the work when done is done once and for all. In economics this is not the case and to convert a model into a quantitative formula is to destroy its usefulness as an instrument of thought . . . by filling in figures which one can be quite sure will not apply next time, so far from increasing the value of his instrument he has decreased it.'[4]

On the other hand the sense of crisis in the discipline had its salutary effects. It sharpened the challenge faced by those who were already aware of the huge gaps in their data resources and of the weakness of their basic theoretical equipment. It acted as a stimulus to the now large core of research economists who were actively committed to the advancement of a rigorous and technically advanced economic science. It contributed to an enlargement of intellectual horizons by breaking down the tunnel vision of a dominant orthodoxy and by encouraging economists to take a critical interest, not only in alternative models of the economic system, but also in potentially relevant ideas spinning off from contemporary research in other disciplines (for example, other social sciences, or mathematics, or history, or philosophy of science or ethics).

One of the most conspicuous features of mid twentieth-century research in economics, for example, has been an enormous increase in the application of advanced mathematical techniques of analysis. Another, more recent, development—less widespread, but potentially important in improving the quality and extending the range of economic understanding—has been a propensity on the part of leading academic theorists to explore and clarify some of the philosophical issues which have so often muddied economic debates conducted across ideological divides. No doubt there was also some diminution in the arrogance of economists, though it is fair to say that for most of those at the cutting edge of the advancement of economic knowledge, the virtue of professional humility has been respected ever since the late nineteenth-century crisis in economic theory. Keynes, for example, was paraphrasing Marshall when he asserted in the 1922 editorial introduction to a new series of student texts that: 'The Theory of Economics does not furnish a body of settled conclusions immediately applicable to a policy. It is a method rather than a doctrine, an apparatus of the mind, a technique of thinking which helps its possessor to draw correct conclusions.' It is significant, moreover, that the citations for the Nobel Prizes in Economic Sciences (first awarded in 1969) do not describe a stream of definitive discoveries. Each in effect acclaims some economist for outstanding contributions to the improvement of the scientific machinery of his discipline.

That advances in economic knowledge are typically no more than tentative, exploratory, or conjectural, that their explanations are rarely robust, and that their most successful predictions are only roughly right, is not in dispute among the professionals. When defending their theoretical innovations or empirical discoveries they often pretend to more conviction than they actually have—justifiably enough in communications addressed to colleagues who can be expected to respond critically to the intellectual challenge. What is not within their sights is the kind of consensual, cumulatively progressive, and operationally relevant advances in objective knowledge that their counterparts in the natural sciences may aspire to achieve. This sets economists apart from the other scientific experts on whom governments may call for advice. 'Ideally', according to the natural scientist John Ziman, 'the general body of scientific knowledge should consist of facts and principles which are firmly established and accepted without serious doubt by an overwhelming majority of well-informed scientists.'[5]

There are of course obvious reasons why economic knowledge falls short of this ideal. The most obvious is that the economic system changes its strategic parameters through time in ways that the natural universe does not. Indeed, patterns of economic behaviour may sometimes adapt to individual agents' perceptions of what contemporary theory predicts for them. Another reason is that the hierarchy of problems stacked up for each generation of research economists is determined at least as much by the current priorities of policymakers, the urgent consumers of economic knowledge, as by the issues currently identified as fundamental by scholars engaged in scientific research programmes.

The result is that the ultimate validators of much of contemporary economic research are not academics and specialists professionally equipped by training to criticize, test, and apply new theories and arguments, or to confirm and interpret new observations, but the politicians, civil servants, journalists, business men, and others who are interested in their potential for clarifying, or informing, or justifying choices between, practical policy options relevant to today's socio-politico-economic problems. This is especially so when research funds are limited and largely controlled by government agencies. True, many of today's consumers of economic research results are sufficiently educated or have sufficient relevant practical experience to be able to evaluate the professionals's explanations critically and intelligently. Nevertheless, at that misty interface between carefully qualified explanations and predictions on the one hand, and commonsensical accounts and policy prescriptions on the other, the scope for distorting what economists imprecisely know into what politicians and ideologues are determined to justify is vast.

The events that brought inflation to the top of the agenda of governments in capitalist market economies in the course of the 1970s destroyed their residual confidence in the efficacy of demand management for reducing unemployment and stimulating productivity growth and persuaded them that attempts to control the foreign exchange values of their currencies were not only ineffectual but potentially harmful in their side effects. Politicians and officials were then faced with a radical problem shift, with a fierce libertarian reaction against centralized economic controls and with a growing propensity on the part of their economic advisers to stress the long-run equilibrating properties of an unfettered price mechanism. They badly needed a new set of rules to guide their economic policies.

There was actually more than one set on offer. At the start it was the monetarists who seemed to meet the need. They had the advantage that they were not hawking a novel or unfamiliar doctrine and that it was focused almost exclusively on the inflation problem. Their reasoning had the necessary quality of seeming lucid and uncomplicated to non-economists and it could easily be shown to be consistent with apparently incontrovertible empirical evidence. Their rules were superficially simple to explain and to operate and were congenial to governments anxious to shed as many as possible of the responsibilities that their predecessors had proved incompetent to handle.

Basically, the monetarist rules implied confining monetary policy to the automatic (non-discretionary) function of keeping money supply growing in line with the volume of transactions, of using fiscal policy largely if not entirely for micro-economic objectives (for example, stimulating incentives to produce or redistributing incomes between socio-economic groups) and restoring a large measure of competition to the market place by dismantling government regulations on private enterprise and restoring nationalized industries to the private sector.

In practice the rules were not as easy to apply as appeared on paper. There are no unambiguous measures of the money supply, for example, and, as it turned out, there is scope for the authorities to exercise considerable discretion in switching between alternative definitions or instruments and in choosing how fast or how heavily to intervene. Nevertheless, there was a veritable rush among western governments to adopt avowedly monetarist macro-economic policies and related neo-classical micro-economic policies, and to reject Keynesian recipes.

It would of course be misleading to suggest that most governments and their economic advisers were converted to the undiluted monetarist doctrines overnight. Belief in the 'naturally' self-regulating properties of the modern market economy does not run deep and it is in the nature of twentieth-century governments—even those who profess to abhor activist economic policies—to intervene purposefully and selectively in the economic system. However, the fact that Keynesian economics had been publicly discredited by its association with the failures of economic management and had lost the intellectual conviction that attached to doctrinal solidarity, by splintering into sub-schools, gave a distinctly monetarist bias to the policy decisions taken (even by left-wing governments) in the late 1970s and the 1980s. Moreover, a rift had developed and seemed to be widening between the economic scientists who were self-consciously committed to researches aimed at effecting fundamental repairs in the theories, analytical techniques, and empirical resources of their discipline and the economic consultants who were primarily concerned to offer advice and critical comment on current decision making—whether to government, business, trade unions, international organizations, or to the public at large through the media.

In part this is due to the increasingly specialized and technical character of modern economic research. Many of today's highly formalized academic articles that fill the learned journals, for example, are incomprehensible (or uninteresting) not only to rank and file applied economists (for instance, to members of the government economic service or economic journalists) but also to academic economists in other specialisms. The dangers of a gulf emerging between the economists who intend to push out the frontiers of economic knowledge and the political economists aiming to supply instant, easily intelligible professional advice to practical decision makers are twofold: first, that the latter may be ill-informed about the most apposite and up-to-date research findings in their own discipline; and second, that the frontiersmen will be insufficiently inclined to develop their enquiries to the point where they would be accessible and useful to those who might be interested in applying them to contemporary problems.

In the last analysis, of course, governments choose their own economic experts and have always been selective about whom they will listen to and what advice they will accept from the chosen few. Since the economic arguments are not the only ones to be taken into account in the process of policy formulation, they are right to do so.

What appears to be a new development—arising out of the situations in which the expertise of leading economists can be brushed aside as questionable or of dubious relevance—is the propensity of modern governments to invent their own bastard economics to justify their policies. Certain conservative administrations of the 1980s, for example, have appealed to something called 'supply-side economics' (to distinguish it from Keynesian 'demand-side economics'?) which has been used to justify a policy of cutting taxes (at the expense usually of welfare expenditures and sometimes even to the extent of incurring budget deficits), on the grounds that this will offer the incentives needed to stimulate additional investment, output, and employment.

However, this may not be such a new development as it seems. There is a long tradition of governments being more open to influence from what the 1985 Reith Lecturer, David Henderson, called 'do-it-yourself-economics' (i.e. the intuitive ideas of laymen, informed by casual empiricism and even more casual theorizing) in preference to systematically designed economic models embodying reputable research results.

References

Chapter 2

1. Albert Einstein, Foreword to Stillman Drake's translation of *Galileo's Dialogue Concerning the Two Chief World Systems* (1953).
2. Sir William Petty, *The Political Anatomy of Ireland*, in C.H. Hull (ed.), *The Economic Writings of Sir William Petty*, vol. i (1899), p. 128.
3. *Political Arithmetick*, in Hull, op. cit., vol. i, p. 244.
4. *A Treatise of Taxes and Contributions*, in Hull, op. cit., p. 30.
5. Peter Laslett (ed.), *Locke's Two Treatises on Government* (1970).
6. John Locke, *Consequences of the lowering of interest and raising the value of money*, appended to the 1870 edn. of J. R. McCulloch's *Principles of Political Economy*.

Chapter 3

1. Richard Cantillon, *Essay on the Nature of Trade in General*, translated for the Royal Economic Society by Henry Higgs (1931), p. 321.
2. Ibid., pp. 215–18.
3. Ibid., p. 43.
4. Sir James Steuart, *An Inquiry into the Principles of Political Economy* (1767), ed. Andrew Skinner for the Scottish Economic Society (1966), vol. i, p. 142.
5. Ibid., p. 143.
6. Ibid., pp. 323–4. Itals in the original.

Chapter 4

1. Quoted by Robert Brown in *The Nature of Social Laws from Machiavelli to Mill* (1984).
2. Adam Smith, *An Inquiry into the Nature and Causes of the Wealth of Nations*, ed. R.H. Campbell and A.S. Skinner, vol. i (1976), p. 428.
3. Ibid., vol. ii, p. 663.
4. Ibid., p. 687.
5. Ibid., vol. i, p. 540.
6. Ibid., p. 454.

7. Ibid., p. 456.
8. Ibid., p. 46.
9. Adam Smith, *The Theory of Moral Sentiments*, ed. D. D. Raphael and A. L. Macfie (1976), pp. 233–4.
10. *Wealth of Nations*, op. cit., vol. ii, pp. 687–8.
11. Ibid. p. 471.

Chapter 5

1. Steuart (ed. Skinner) op. cit., vol. i, p. 32.
2. T. R. Malthus, *Principles of Political Economy* (1820), reprinted in P. Sraffa (ed.), *Works and Correspondence of David Ricardo*, vol. ii (1966), p. 12.
3. Ibid., p. 5.
4. D. Ricardo, *On the Principles of Political Economy and Taxation* (1821), reprinted in P. Sraffa (ed.), op. cit., vol. i (1970), p. 388.
5. Ibid., p. 392.

Chapter 6

1. J. S. Mill, *A System of Logic, Ratiocinative and Inductive*, Toronto edn. ed. J. M. Robson (1973), p. 384.
2. Ibid., p. 901.
3. Ibid., p. 906.
4. J. S. Mill, *Essays on Economics and Society*, Toronto edn. ed. J. M. Robson (1967), p. 322.
5. K. Marx, *A Contribution to the Critique of Political Economy* (1971 edn.), ed. and introduced by Maurice Dobb.
6. K. Marx, *Capital* (1887), reprinted 1970, p. 20.
7. Ibid., p. 372.
8. Mill, *Logic*, op. cit.

Chapter 7

1. J. M. Keynes, 'William Stanley Jevons', reprinted in *Essays in Biography*, vol. x of *The Collected Writings of J. M. Keynes*, Royal Economic Society edn. (1972), p. 131.
2. Quoted by J. M. Keynes in his 1924 Memoir of Alfred Marshall, reprinted in *Essays in Biography*, op. cit., p. 171.
3. A. Marshall, 'The Present Position of Economics' (1885), reprinted in A. C. Pigou (ed.), *Memorials of Alfred Marshall* (1925), p. 159.

4. A. Marshall, 'The Old Generation of Economists and the New', *Quarterly Journal of Economics* (1897), pp. 116–17.
5. D. H. Macgregor, 'Marshall and his Book', *Economica* (Nov. 1942), p. 314.

Chapter 8

1. Passage reprinted in J. M. Keynes, *Essays in Persuasion*, vol. ix of the Royal Economic Society edn. of *The Collected Writings of J. M. Keynes* (1972), p. 75.
2. Ibid., p. 288.
3. J. M. Keynes, *A Treatise on Money* (1930), vol. i, p. 133.
4. J. M. Keynes, *Essays in Persuasion*, op. cit., p. 298.
5. Ibid., p. 245.
6. Ibid., pp. 90–1.
7. Quoted by J. M. Keynes, ibid., p. 115.
8. J. M. Keynes, *The General Theory of Employment, Interest and Money* (1936), p. 3.
9. Ibid.
10. Ibid., pp. 246–7.
11. Ibid., p. 373.

Chapter 9

1. A. W. Phillips, 'The relationship between unemployment and the rate of change of money wages in the United Kingdom, 1861–1957', *Economica* (1958).
2. See F. W. Paish, *Studies in an Inflationary Economy* (1962) for the thesis underlying this prescription.
3. M. Friedman (ed.), *Studies in the Quantity Theory of Money* (1956), pp. 3–21.
4. In correspondence with R. F. Harrod dated July 1938, vol. xiv, *Collected Writings of J. M. Keynes*, op. cit.
5. J. M. Ziman, *Reliable Knowledge* (1978), p. 6.

Further reading

There are now a great many good histories of economic thought, each written from an individual perspective and for a particular purpose. Joseph Schumpeter's monumental *History of Economic Analysis* (1954) is an invaluable work of reference; although it contains some highly idiosyncratic judgements and finishes in the 1940s, it is still the most brilliant, erudite, stylish, epigrammatic, and, above all, comprehensive history of economic thought available. Mark Blaug's *Economic Theory in Retrospect* (3rd edn. 1974), written from the perspective of a contemporary economic theorist, abstracts from the philosophical, political, social, and institutional background and evaluates past economic theories in terms of their contribution to current mainstream economic orthodoxy in North America and the UK. In contrast, my own *Evolution of Economic Ideas* (1978) traces the process of change in the ideas of successive generations of economists and treats more fully some of the theories and arguments sketched in the present volume.

A number of seminal works are referred to in the text of this volume. Readers who are interested in a particular economist would be well advised to go back to primary sources before their palates are jaded or their judgements stereotyped by over-exposure to secondary literature. For most of the major economists there exists a modern edition of their *magna opera* introduced by an evaluation or commentary by a leading specialist. Examples are: the editorial introductions to the Glasgow, 1976 edition of Adam Smith's *Inquiry into the Nature and Causes of the Wealth of Nations* (ed. R. H. Campbell and A. S. Skinner) or *The Theory of Moral Sentiments* (ed. D. D. Raphael and A. L. Macfie), Andrew Skinner's introduction to Sir James Steuart's *Inquiry into the Principles of Political Œconomy* (1966); Donald Winch's introduction to David Ricardo's *Principles of Political Economy and Taxation* (1973). For Richard Cantillon there is a Royal Economic Society reprint of his *Essai sur la Nature du Commerce en Générale* (1931) containing both the French and the English versions together with a general introduction by Henry Higgs and a reprinted review article by W. S. Jevons, 'Richard Cantillon and the Nationality of Political Economy', originally published in the *Contemporary Review*. It is worth noting also that Keynes's *Essays in Biography*, republished in 1972 as vol. x of the *Collected Writings of John Maynard Keynes*, contains significant evaluations of a number of economists, including T. R. Malthus, W. S. Jevons, and Alfred Marshall, as well as of Isaac Newton and Albert Einstein.

A selection of relatively recent books which will carry the reader further and deeper on some of the wide variety of themes touched on in this volume are listed below by chapters.

2 Political economy in the shadow of the scientific revolution

Joyce O. Appleby, *Economic Thought and Ideology in Seventeenth Century England*, 1978.

I. Bernard Cohen, *The Newtonian Revolution*, 1980.

C. C. Gillespie, *The Edge of Objectivity*, 1960.

J. K. Horsefield, *British Monetary Experiments 1650–1710*, 1960.

John Dunn, *Locke*, 1984.

3 The search for scientific principles

Marion Bowley, *Studies in the History of Economic Theory before 1870*, 1973.

H. Montgomery Hyde, *John Law: The History of an Honest Adventurer*, 1969.

Douglas Vickers, *Studies in the Theory of Money 1690–1776*, 1960.

4 The system-builders

Michel Foucault, *The Order of Things: An Archaeology of the Human Sciences*, 1970.

R. L. Meek, *The Economics of Physiocracy*, 1963.

G. S. Rousseau and Roy Porter (eds.), *The Ferment of Knowledge: Studies in the Historiography of Eighteenth Century Science*, 1980.

Donald Winch, *Adam Smith's Politics*, 1978.

5 The dismal scientists

F. W. Fetter, *The Development of British Monetary Orthodoxy 1789–1875*, 1976.

D. P. O'Brien, *The Classical Economists*, 1978.

6 The search for a scientific consensus

G. Duncan, *Marx and Mill: Two Views of Social Conflict and Harmony*, 1976.
A. Ryan, *J. S. Mill*, 1974.

7 From political economy to economic science

R. D. Collison Black, A. W. Coats, and C. D. W. Goodwin, *The Marginal Revolution in Economics*, 1973.
Stefan Collini, Donald Winch, and John Burrow, *That Noble Science of Politics: A Study in Nineteenth Century Intellectual History*, 1983.
John Maloney, *Marshall, Orthodoxy and the Professionalisation of Economics*, 1985.
Dov Ospovat, *The Development of Darwin's Theory: Natural History, Natural Theology and Natural Selection, 1838–1859*, 1981.

8 Economic science in an unstable world economy

Milo Keynes (ed.), *Essays on John Maynard Keynes*, 1975.
D. E. Moggridge, *Keynes*, 1976.
G. L. S. Shackle, *The Years of High Theory, 1926–1939*, 1967.
Donald Winch, *Economics and Policy: A Historical Study*, 1969.

9 The rise and fall of economic management

F. T. Blackaby, *British Economic Policy 1960–74*, 1978.
A. K. Cairncross, *Years of Recovery, British Economic Policy 1945–51*, 1985.
J. C. R. Dow, *The Management of the British Economy 1945–60*, 1964.
David Henderson, *Innocence and Design, The Influence of Economic Ideas on Policy*, 1986.

Index

OXFORD

MORE OXFORD PAPERBACKS

Details of a selection of other books follow. A complete list of Oxford Paperbacks, including The World's Classics, Twentieth-Century Classics, OPUS, Past Masters, Oxford Authors, Oxford Shakespeare, and Oxford Paperback Reference, is available in the UK from the General Publicity Department, Oxford University Press (JN), Walton Street, Oxford OX2 6DP.

In the USA, complete lists are available from the Paperbacks Marketing Manager, Oxford University Press, 200 Madison Avenue, New York, NY 10016.

Oxford Paperbacks are available from all good bookshops. In case of difficulty, customers in the UK can order direct from Oxford University Press Bookshop, 116 High Street, Oxford, Freepost, OX1 4BR, enclosing full payment. Please add 10 per cent of published price for postage and packing.

THE ECONOMY OF ENGLAND, 1450–1750

D. C. Coleman

Two centuries ago the Industrial Revolution began transforming the economy of England into the form in which we know it today. But what sort of economy did England have in preceding centuries? Professor Coleman gives us an account of three centuries of English economic life, stretching from the Wars of the Roses almost to the accession of George III. He never allows us to forget that the economic world in which the men and women of the day lived and died was only one aspect of their historical context. And just as he puts the economy of England into its social and political setting, so he also presents it in its changing relationship with the economy of Europe and the wider world. In this last connection the period from 1650 to 1750, rarely treated as a whole, receives particular emphasis as marking the economic divergence of England from the Continent.

'Professor Coleman brings a welcome freshness of learning and originality of style to the subject-matter which makes this work an excellent statement of the more temperate position which lies between 'old' and 'new' economic historians.' Barry Supple, *Times Literary Supplement*

An OPUS book

CONTEMPORARY INTERNATIONAL THEORY AND THE BEHAVIOUR OF STATES

Joseph Frankel

This book provides a brief survey of the major theoretical approaches to international relations: systems analysis, integration theory, the action of states, and states in interaction. In a concluding chapter some of these approaches are applied in a case study of the relations between Britain and the European Economic Community.

HONG KONG IN SEARCH OF A FUTURE

Joseph Y. S. Cheng

During the past few years, the future of Hong Kong has been the subject of heated debate within the Hong Kong community as well as internationally. Widespread discussion and intense speculation have resulted in the voicing of a broad spectrum of opinion.

Hong Kong in Search of a Future records this debate. It contains not only official documents and semi-official statements by the Chinese, British and Hong Kong Governments on Hong Kong's future, but also sets out important opinion polls and a representative sample of the views of major groups and the media. A major focus of the book is the visit to China of Margaret Thatcher in September 1982, and the differences revealed during that visit between the Chinese and British Governments on the question of sovereignty and the 'unequal treatise'. With China refusing to compromise, the British Government may well have begun to prepare for the worst, while the citizens of Hong Kong have grown increasingly uneasy as change appears inevitable.

THATCHERISM AND BRITISH POLITICS

The End of Consensus?

Dennis Kavanagh

Mrs Thatcher has cited the breaking of the post-war political consensus, established with the support of dominant groups in the Conservative and Labour parties, as one of her objectives. In this penetrating study of her style and performance, she emerges both as the midwife of the collapse of consensus and also as its product.

STERLING: ITS USE AND MISUSE
A Plea for Moderation
Douglas Jay

Douglas Jay, a former Labour Treasury Minister, presents a compelling history of the pound sterling from its earliest beginnings until the present time, culminating in a remarkable listing of the Retail Price Index for every year (with five exceptions) from 1264 to 1983. In a brilliantly argued and highly controversial final section, he disputes the conventional wisdom of the monetarists, contending that the price of full employment is not escalating inflation. He advocates moderation on both sides of the political fence, concluding that the development of a workable incomes policy could be the solution to Britain's current dilema.

'Young economists should turn off their computers long enough to read Douglas Jay's dazzling new book.' The *Financial Times*

THE REAL WORLD OF DEMOCRACY
C. B. Macpherson

In the Massey Lectures, delivered over the Canadian Broadcasting Corporation in 1965, Professor Macpherson examines what he considers to be three legitimate forms of democracy: the liberal democracy of the West, the kind of democracy practised in the Soviet block countries, and the mass democracy of the newly independent states of Africa and Asia. The work is attractively written and the argument is provocative: it should stimulate discussion on an important subject. At another level it seeks to question the validity of all the acquisitive and competitive motives that have characterized human survival and progress in the past.

THE RISE AND FALL OF ECONOMIC
JUSTICE AND OTHER PAPERS

C. B. Macpherson

Aspects of twentieth-century democracy such as economic justice, human rights, industrial democracy, property, pluralism,
and the roots of liberalism are explored in this book, which
carries further the analyses made in C. B. Macpherson's previous two books. The essays contained in this volume are at
once comparative and historical, and their subject-matter is
wide-ranging.

'The book is wide in scope . . . For those concerned with the
notion of property and its role in society this is a valuable
addition.' *British Book News*

THE ORIGINS OF TRADE UNION POWER

Henry Phelps Brown

Professor Phelps Brown has thoroughly revised and updated
his history of trade unionism in Britain—described by the
Guardian as 'his masterwork'—for this new edition.

'a brilliant, magisterial valediction to a lifetime's study of Britain's industrial relations . . . it deserves to become a classic'
New Society

'a wise, and an instructive book. For every topical question
concerning trade unions this book provides the historical background as well as reflections which cannot be pushed aside.'
British Journal of Industrial Relations

DEMOCRACY AT WORK

Tom Schuller

Should people play a significant part in decisions affecting their working lives? *Democracy at Work* takes a fresh look at the controversial question of industrial democracy in the light of recent changes in the structure of employment and in the balance of decision-making.

'This short but elegantly written book airs a number of important issues and points to the narrowness of much of the current perspectives in Britain on worker participation.' *Times Higher Education Supplement*

MARX'S SOCIAL THEORY

Terrell Carver

Why has Marx had such a wide-ranging impact on our intellectual and political life? Terrell Carver presents a new analysis of what Marx called the 'guiding thread' of his studies, which is set out in his 1859 preface *A Critique of Political Economy*, together with an important autobiographical sketch, which the author reanalyses in this book. He argues that Marx's 'production theory of society and social change' is analogous to Darwin's work in a hitherto unnoticed way and is just as scientific. He assesses the central difficulties encountered by the theory, and shows that it sprang from a desire not simply to interpret the world, but to change it.

THE WORKSHOP OF THE WORLD

British Economic History 1820–1880 2/e

J. D. Chambers

A vivid and authoritative account of Britain's economic life between 1820 and 1880, beginning when the country was in the transitional phase from a primarily agricultural and commercial economy to a modern industrial State. At the end of the period Britain was the world's banker, trader, and collier, and a competitor with other nations whom she herself had materially assisted.

'. . . refreshing and relevant reading. As an introduction it could hardly be bettered.' *The Times*

An *OPUS* book

THE WAY PEOPLE WORK

Job Satisfaction and the Challenge of Change

Christine Howarth

What makes a job satisfying? How can we improve the quality of working life? Does greater job satisfaction mean greater efficiency?

These are some of the many questions which both managers and employees must ask themselves (and each other) if the organizations for which they work are to have any chance of success in today's harsh economic climate. Christine Howarth, who has many years' experience as an independent management consultant, has written this book as a *practical* guide to human relationships in employment.

An OPUS book

MAIN CURRENTS OF MARXISM

Leszek Kolakowski

Volume 1: The Founders

In this first volume, Leszek Kolakowski examines the origins of Marxism, tracing its descent, from the neo-Platonists through Hegel and the Enlightenment. He analyses the development of Marx's thought and shows its divergence from other forms of socialism.

'the most commanding, the most decisive, the most properly passionate and yet also . . . the most accessible account of Marxism that we now have. It is a work of surpassing lucidity and power, of the sharpest and most sensitive judgement, of a far finer quality than almost all of that with which it deals. It is, in short, a masterpiece.'

Times Higher Educational Supplement

A THEORY OF ECONOMIC HISTORY

John Hicks

Economists are inclined to think of the market economy as always existing, just developing or 'growing'; historians (and anthropologists) know very well that that is not the case. An attempt is made in this book to build a bridge between their opposing views. Its subject is the evolution of the market economy, its forms and institutions; an evolution which has great things to its credit, but has many darker sides. Some of the dark sides—slavery and usury and the darker aspects of colonization—are given considerable attention. The discussion culminates in an analysis of the Industrial Revolution. Examples drawn from four thousand years of history illustrate this celebrated study.

HOW TO BEAT UNEMPLOYMENT

Richard Layard

Unemployment is the major social problem of our time. In Britain it is now as high as it was in the 1930s; many people doubt whether it can be reduced. The obvious remedy of increasing public spending appears to cause an undesirable increase in inflation as well. This book investigates the causes of unemployment and makes strong and detailed recommendations for reducing it, expanding output, and containing inflation. The strategy includes creating jobs to suit the abilities of the unemployed, training the less skilled, reintroducing an incomes policy, and defending the value of the pound.

CAPITALIST DEMOCRACY IN BRITAIN

Ralph Miliband

How has Britain succeeded in avoiding violent political conflict on a wide scale since the suffrage was extended in 1867? Ralph Miliband suggests that the answer lies in a political system that has proved capable of controlling pressure from below by absorbing it. He illustrates his theories with reference to recent political events.

'Miliband's special contribution has made him our foremost Marxist political theorist.' *New Statesman*